Living & Learning with Children

Living & Learning with Children

by Paula Jorde
illustrated by Dennis Lee

ACROPOLIS BOOKS LTD.
Washington, D.C. 20009

Acropolis Books Ltd.
Colortone Building, 2400 17th St. N.W.
Washington, D.C. 20009

Printed in the United States of America by
Colortone Press Creative Graphics, Inc.
Washington, D.C. 20009

Library of Congress Cataloging in Publication Data

Jorde, Paula.
  Living & learning with children

  Publishd in 1976 under title: The kids do it book.
    1. Education, Preschool—Handbooks, manuals,
etc.   2. Creative activities and seat work—Handbooks,
manuals, etc. I. Lee, Dennis. II. Title.
LB1140.2.J67 1976   649'.5   76-796
ISBN 0-912078-47-2

To Kirsten and Brenda,

who have added so much joy to my life.

CONTENTS CONTENTS CONTENTS CONTENTS CONTENTS

Dear Parent and Teacher,

Your role in shaping the physical, social, intellectual and emotional development of young children is crucial. The learning experiences that children encounter in their early, formative years have a great impact on their overall self-esteem and later success in school. In a sense, however, your role as "teacher" is an easy one, because young children are so eager and anxious to learn. Their natural curiosity drives them to question, explore, and discover more about the world in which they live.

I'm sure you are continually amazed (and at times annoyed) with their unending search for answers. But it is this desire to understand and to make sense out of the unknown that motivates children to reach out and learn more about life. What children need, however, is direction and encouragement. This is where the relationship of trust and support you have so carefully nurtured comes into play. Children look to you as a vital source of knowledge and guidance. LIVING & LEARNING WITH CHILDREN was written to help you in this role of guiding children to become successful learners.

Because you know your child or the children in your classroom better than anyone else, it is up to you to select activities that are appropriate to their age and ability level. In other words, use your judgment and select activities that will not pressure or frustrate the child, yet will encourage thinking and learning. The wording you use to present a project is also very important and should vary, of course, according to the child's age and ability.

While the ideas on the following pages are appropriate for both home and school, teachers reading LIVING & LEARNING WITH CHILDREN may desire additional activities for young children in a group setting. To fill this need, I have included a special teacher's supplement at the end of the book that is jam-packed with group activities for small groups.

A word about metrics: You will notice that all the measurements in LIVING & LEARNING WITH CHILDREN are given in metric units as well as their English equivalents. I hope that as you do the activities with young children you will use the metric measurements exclusively. This will be excellent practice for the children, but will also assist you in learning to convert to the new system. Our goal is to help children begin to "think metric" starting with their earliest experiences with measurement activities.

When playing some of the learning games in this book, keep in mind the following suggestions:

Be Patient. Children need a lot of time to think. When they are pressured to hurry up or perform faster, the game will no longer be fun. Try to avoid giving hints or answers; let the child learn to think independently. And if the child makes a mistake, don't make a big deal out of it. Try to convey that learning involves making mistakes and encourage the child to try again. Avoid creating a "testing" or evaluating atmosphere. The best way to develop an instant rapport is to dig in and try some of these games and activities yourself — you'll be surprised what fun it can be to let go and let the "child" in you take over.

Praise, Praise, Praise. Recognize the child's accomplishments, no matter how small. Select activities that will build confidence and insure success. Remember, *children are seldom motivated by failure; only success breeds more success.*

Be Flexible. If the child seems frustrated by a certain activity because it is too difficult, by all means STOP! Do something else. Also, don't drag a game on forever. When the child begins to wiggle or lose interest, that's the time to put the activity away. Try not to coax or show disappointment. Learning should be fun. If you turn these games into a chore, children will quickly become turned off and uncooperative. So relax and have fun. If they're not interested in working with you one day, don't take it as a personal insult. Try again another day.

Improvise, Explore and Invent new games yourself. The ideas in LIVING & LEARNING WITH CHILDREN are only suggestions. If children want to change the rules of a game, great! They should be encouraged to think of variations for other activities too. The materials required for the ideas in this book are inexpensive and simple to use. Most can be scrounged from neighborhood merchants or found in discarded junk. If you don't have a suggested item, think of other "litterbug materials" you might use as substitutes. You'll be surprised what wild and wonderful imaginative powers both you and your children have for inventing new and creative ways to learn.

Good Luck and Have Fun!

Paula Jorde

I believe in children —
little ones, big ones,
chubby ones, thin ones.

There is faith in their eyes,
love in their touch,
hope in their attitude.

sensory awareness

Children learn about the world through their five senses—they see, hear, smell, touch and taste. When they are given the opportunity to manipulate and explore things in their own way, their awareness and understanding of the world is enriched. There is much you can do, however, to help your child become more sensitive to the experiences s/he encounters.

The activities in this section are designed to sharpen your child's senses. After doing some of these activities with your child, you should take every opportunity to encourage discussion about his or her experiences in terms of *all* the senses. For instance, if you have a picnic on the beach you can ask your child to describe how the air smells, how the salt water tastes, how the crashing waves sound, how the sand feels or how many seagulls s/he sees. Your child's vocabulary will expand and, more importantly, his or her appreciation of life will be enriched by an increased awareness of the sensory environment.

hearing

The Ticking Timer

Set a kitchen cooking timer for about five minutes then hide it somewhere in the house. Let your child hunt down the ticking sound before the bell goes off.

Listening Walk

Take a walk around your neighborhood and write down all the sounds you and your child hear. For example, you might hear the wind blowing, birds singing, an airplane passing overhead or a car horn.

Flip top bandage box

35 MM film can

Shake a Sound

Collect eight or ten 35 mm film cans or flip-top bandage boxes. Fill two of them with rice, two with thumbtacks, two with buttons and two with water. Mix them up. Your child will have fun trying to match the different sounds. You might also use paper clips, pebbles, popcorn or toothpicks to fill the cans.

Hear and Do

Give your child three simple commands such as "Walk to the table, turn around twice, and sit on the chair." After she has mastered a certain number of commands, make them more difficult and increase the number.

Finish It

Recite part of a nursery rhyme and have your child fill in a word, phrase or line using the rhyming words as a clue. For example:

> Humpty Dumpty sat on a wall,
> Humpty Dumpty had a great _____ .

or

> Hickory Dickory dock,
> The mouse ran up the _____ .

2

Rhyming Riddles

Make up some riddles for a particular family of rhyming words and encourage your child to think of the answers by using rhyming clues. For example, here are some simple riddles for two different rhyming families (sat, hat, fat, bat, cat, rat and look, book, hook, crook, brook):

I'm thinking of a word that sounds like sat,
I wear it on my head, so it must be a ———— .

I'm thinking of a word that sounds like hat,
If I'm the opposite of skinny, I must be ———— .

I'm thinking of a word that sounds like fat,
When I play baseball, I must use a ———— .

I'm thinking of a word that sounds like bat,
It says meow, so it must be a ———— .

I'm thinking of a word that rhymes with look,
When I want to read, I open a ———— .

I'm thinking of a word that rhymes with book,
To hang up my coat I use a ———— .

I'm thinking of a word that rhymes with hook,
I use my eyes to see and ———— .

I'm thinking of a word that rhymes with look,
I use my pots and pans to ———— .

I'm thinking of a word that rhymes with cook,
Sometimes a thief is called a ———— .

I'm thinking of a word that rhymes with crook,
A small stream is called a ———— .

What Is It?

Ask your child to close his eyes. Make some familiar sounds and let him try to identify each one. For example, you might knock on the door, drop a pencil, clap your hands, snap your fingers, or bounce a ball.

Paper Cup Telephones

Punch a hole in the bottom of two paper cups or juice cans. Connect the two cups with a piece of string about 6 meters (20 feet) long. To keep the string from pulling through the holes, you might want to tie it to a piece of toothpick on the inside of the cup. Talk and listen to your child making sure the string is kept straight.

touching

Mystery Bag

Collect several different objects and put them in an old pillow case. Your child will enjoy reaching into the bag, feeling an object and trying to guess what it is using only her sense of touch. Ask her questions about how each object feels. Is it soft? smooth? rough? hard? round? Does it have edges? Does it feel tickly? prickly? slippery? fuzzy? squishy? or fluffy? Some things you might want to include in the bag: a toothbrush, a rubber ball, a marble, a piece of sandpaper, a piece of rope, a small book or spoon.

How Does It Feel?

While your child is getting himself dressed in the morning, have him talk to you about how his different clothes feel. Are they soft? scratchy? stiff? limp? fuzzy? bumpy? or smooth?

Textured Rubbings

Place a piece of paper on top of different surfaces like tile, cement, frosted glass, or the radiator. Then rub on top of the paper with the flat side of a crayon.

Find It

Take a walk around your house and ask your child to find something that is hard, soft, rough or smooth. Something that is made of wood, plastic, metal, paper, glass, rubber, feathers or leather. Something that is hot, cold, sharp, dull, wet or dry.

Feel It On Your Toes

Your child might enjoy walking barefoot across different textured materials like a rug, a piece of paper, some wood, the sidewalk or some mud. Encourage her to describe how each different surface feels on her feet.

smelling

Sniff and Tell

Put into different baby jars: cloves, mint, flower petals, sawdust, ammonia, onions, cinnamon, cocoa, garlic, detergent, coffee, tobacco or anything else that has a strong odor. Blindfold your child. He will have fun trying to guess the contents of each jar by sniff alone. Encourage him to describe each of the odors . . . . does it remind him of a place he has visited or a particular food he has eaten?

Nose Walk

Walk around the neighborhood with your child and write down all the things you smell with your nose, such as gasoline fumes, flowers, a cake baking, freshly cut grass, garbage or pond water.

Smells I Like; Smells I Don't Like

Your child might want to look through a magazine and cut out pictures of things that are pleasant to smell and things that aren't. She can then paste these in a scrapbook that has been divided into two sections.

5

seeing

Observation Walk

Take a walk around the neighborhood with your child and play simple observation games. On one day you might see how many things he can find that are a particular color . . . a green car, a green bottle, a green roof, green grass. On another day he might try to find as many things as he can that have wheels and move . . . a wagon, a bicycle, a car or a bus.

What Did You See?

Hold up a detailed picture for a few moments and let your child study it. Put it away and ask her questions about the picture. "How many children were there in the picture?" "Was it daytime or night time?" Switch and let her ask you questions about a picture you look at.

I Spy

Look around the room, select an object and then describe it to your child. Give him one clue at a time until he guesses what it is. Then it is his turn to give clues to you.

Color Run

Call out a color and let your child run to touch something that is that color. Then let her call out a color for you to touch. Talk about the different shades of a color as you compare the things you touch.

What's Missing?

Put several objects on a table and let your child study them for a few minutes. Have him close his eyes while you remove one of the items. When he opens his eyes, have him guess what is missing. Now it's your turn.

tasting

Have a Tasting Party

Put several different foods on a plate and describe each as you and your child eat it. Is it sweet? salty? sour? tasteless? spicy? bitter? awful? or delicious? For example, try a saltine cracker, a piece of bread, lemon juice, salt water, sugar water, plain water, raisins, a pretzel, a marshmallow or a sour pickle.

Taster's Test

Blindfold your child and give her several different things to taste. See if she can figure out what they are by taste alone.

Tastes I Like; Tastes I Don't Like

Have your child make a scrapbook with two different sections. In the first section he can paste pictures from magazines of things he really likes to eat. In the second section he can paste pictures of things he'd rather not eat.

Yummy Toothpaste

Your child will enjoy making her own toothpaste by mixing 15 ml (1 tbsp.) baking soda, 5 ml (1 tsp.) salt and 5 ml (1 tsp.) of her favorite flavoring like vanilla, almond or peppermint. To keep fresh, store in a jar.

sensory awareness··

For the adult:

Liepmann, L. *Your Child's Sensory World* (New York: Dial Press, 1973).

Maxwell, Margaret John. *Listening Games* (Washington, D.C.: Acropolis 1981).

Wilt, Joy, and Hurn, Gwen. *Listen* (Waco, Texas: Creative Resources, 1978). Imaginative activities that build sensory awareness. Other titles available in this series: *Look; Touch!; Taste and Smell.* All are excellent for use at home or in the classroom

For the child:

Alika. *My Five Senses* (Crowell, 1972). A good introduction to the senses.

Alika. *My Hands* (Crowell, 1962).

Borten, Helen. *Do You Hear What I Hear?* (Abelard-Schuman, 1959). Listening games.

Borten, Helen. *Do You See What I See?* (Abelard-Schuman, 1959).

Brown, Margaret Wise. *Noisy Book* (Harper & Row, 1976). Yes, it's okay to be noisy sometimes, too!

Cameron, Polly. *I Can't Said the Ant* (Coward-McCann, 1961). Nonsense in rhyme. Kids love it.

Carle, Eric. *The Mixed Up Chameleon* (Crowell, 1975).

Carle, Eric. *The Very Hungry Caterpillar* (William Collins-World Publishing, 1969). Nibble, nibble, yum, yum . . . simply delightful!

Charlip, Remy. *Handtalk* (Parents' Magazine Press, 1974). A simple pictorial presentation of American Sign Language.

Levin, Edna. *Lisa and Her Soundless World* (Human Policy Press, 1974). A very touching story of a deaf child and how she copes.

Martin, Bill. *Brown Bear, Brown Bear, What Do You See?* (Holt, Rinehart & Winston, 1965). The repetitive nature of this book develops visual and auditory memory.

Polland, Barbara Kay. *Feelings: Inside You & Outloud, Too* (Celestial Arts, 1975).

Polland, Barbara Kay. *The Sensible Book* (Celestial Arts, 1973). A celebration of the five senses.

Witte, Pat. *Look Look Book* (Western Publishing, 1961).

Zim, Herbert. *What's Inside Of Me?* (Morrow, 1952).

Zolotow, Charlotte. *If You Listen* (Harper & Row, 1980).

getting ready to read and write

There are many ways you as a parent can prepare your child for reading and writing. Beginning at an early age, read to your child as often as possible. A child will begin to love literature naturally if s/he is introduced to books in a friendly, non-threatening way. The more a child gets involved in books and the more curious s/he becomes about the written word, the greater the chances that s/he will want to learn to read and write.

Remember that story time should be fun for both of you. When you have read a story to your child, let him or her read it back to you. S/he may only be able to "read the pictures," but that's fine. Give a lot of help. Ask questions about the story and point out details in the pictures. Soon your child will begin to pick out familiar words and try to sound them out. Get a library card for your child and make frequent trips to the library. S/he can select interesting books and learn to care for them.

Your role as a model is also very important in the motivational aspects of reading. Parents who enjoy reading convey this attitude to their children. Keep in mind, too, that good language and vocabulary development are essential to good reading. Since good talkers usually make good readers, let your child know that what s/he says is important. If you listen —really listen—your child will gain confidence in his or her ability to communicate and be successful at self-expression.

letter recognition and letter sounds

Eat a Letter

Buy a package of alphabet cereal. Sprinkle a handful of letters on the table. Call out a letter and let your child scramble to find it. If she's right, she gets to eat the letter. After she becomes familiar with the letters, you might want to help her arrange them into names and words she knows. Alphabet soup noodles can also be used if you dip them into hot water, drain, and dry on waxed paper. That way they aren't quite as crunchy to eat.

Coil a Letter

Let your child roll play dough into long coils. (There is a good play dough recipe on page 44) He can then practice forming these coils into the letters of his name. You might want to bake them to make the letters hard. Then he can mix up the letters and practice arranging them in the right order for his name. Or, make the letters out of cookie dough and let your child eat his name.

Sandpaper Letters

To help your child "feel" how the letters of the alphabet are made, cut out the different letters from dark sandpaper and mount on pieces of white shirt-backing cardboard. You can also do this with numbers and shapes.

Lines, Hooks and Humps

Talk about the different letters of the alphabet in terms of their distinguishing features so that your child will be able to identify them more easily. Letters are made up of lines, hooks and humps and are either open or closed. You might want to cut out an assortment of letter parts (long and short lines and big and little humps and hooks) and let your child practice fitting the pieces together to make the different letters of the alphabet.

Salty Letters

Pour some salt into a shallow pan and let your child practice making letters (or numbers) in the salt. You can color the salt by adding a little powdered tempera or colored chalk dust.

Sound Bags

For each letter sound that you and your child are working on, cut out a picture of something that begins with that sound and paste it onto a big paper bag. Your child can then put objects and pictures of things that begin with that sound into the bag. For example, if you are working on the sound for the letter B, you might want to cut out a picture of a bear to paste on the bag and collect things like a bell, bone, bib, box or ball to put in the bag.

Loony Letters

Make a large letter on a piece of paper with a crayon or a felt-tipped marker. Your child will have fun trying to make something unusual out of the letter.

Complete the Sentence

Let your child try to complete riddles by using a particular letter sound as a clue. For example, for the letter B:

> We sleep on a _____ .
> We learn many things by reading _____ .
> A fruit that is long and yellow is a _____ .
> When a child is very young he is called a _____ .

Silly Sentences

Make up several silly sentences and let your child try to pick out all the words in that sentence that begin with a particular letter sound. For example:

> B— *Billy* the *baker baked* a *bar* of soap in the *bottom* of the *birthday* cake. When we ate it we all *blew bubbles.*

Back Tracing

With your finger, trace a letter on your child's back. Have her try to guess what the letter is. Now it's her turn to draw a letter on your back and you try to guess what it is.

Letter Collage

Help your child search through a magazine for the letters that are in his name. Cut out the letters and paste them in order on a piece of paper. Underneath his name he might also want to paste words or pictures that are especially meaningful to him.

word power

Take a Trip

One of the surest ways to expand your child's vocabulary and improve her readiness for reading is to expose her to as many different learning situations as possible. Take her with you to the dry cleaners or shoe repair shop the next time you go. Even a simple errand can be turned into a valuable learning experience. Before you go, talk about what you will see. When you return, talk about what you saw and the people you met. Your child may want to draw a picture about her experience. Encourage her to tell you about the picture. If she wants you to, write a story at the bottom of the paper. Some places you might visit together . . . a park, zoo, museum, bakery, forest, railroad station, car wash, greenhouse, florist, kennel, lumber yard, airport, fish pond, construction site, fire station, police station or book store. Remember, a child's growth in language is directly related to the experiences she has had. Your role in providing those experiences is most important.

Words, Words, Everywhere

Take a walk with your child and write down all the words you see on signs, billboards and buses. He will probably be able to read many of them already like EXIT, DANGER, DO NOT TOUCH, ONE WAY, or KEEP OFF THE GRASS!

Part Of

Say a word or show a picture and let your child tell what it is a part of. For example, a wheel is part of a car, a buckle is part of a belt or a page is part of a book.

Position Words

Find a box large enough for your child to crawl into, then give her a number of instructions that involve understanding position. For example: "Stand *behind* the box." "Sit *inside* the box." "Put the paper *underneath* the box." Also use position words like next to, on top of, in the middle of or outside of.

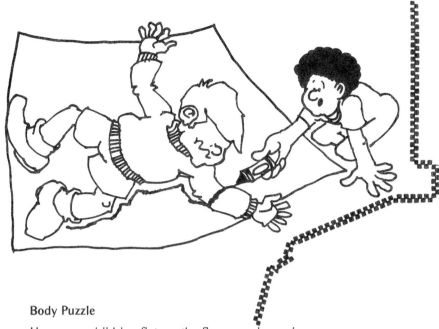

Body Puzzle

Have your child lay flat on the floor on a large piece of butcher paper. Trace around him. He can then color the body form and cut it into different parts. Then as he puts himself together, he can talk about each of the body parts and what its function is.

Body Words

To help your child learn the names of the different parts of the body, give him a series of easy instructions that involve body parts. For example, "Touch your nose." "Shake your leg." "Nod your head." Later you can throw in more difficult body parts and let him guess what they are . . . like ankle, thigh, shin, biceps, knuckles, palm, abdomen, cranium (head-bone), patella (kneecap) or clavicle (collar bone).

Opposites

There are many games you can make up that involve word opposites. When possible try to use real objects or pictures of things to help your child understand what is meant by opposite. Some opposites are:

wet-dry	long-short	walk-run	night-day
old-new	loud-quiet	good-bad	happy-sad
up-down	big-little	near-far	hard-soft
in-out	smile-frown	hot-cold	easy-hard

word recognition

When your child begins to identify and write down words, provide as many opportunities as you can for him to practice his new skills. Let him help you read simple recipes or the directions on packages. Encourage him to make lists of different things he does such as all the television programs he watches in one week, all the food he eats for three days or the household chores he is responsible for. Write notes and messages to your child often and encourage him to do the same. You might also ask him to take down telephone messages for you, write items on the grocery list or keep a "fix-it" list of household items that need repairing.

Tag It

Make a number of cards with different words printed on them . . . like table, chair, bed, desk or radio. Read the words and let your child attach the cards to the appropriate piece of furniture with masking tape. It won't be long before she'll be able to shuffle the cards and place them on the right objects all by herself.

How Do You Feel?

Help your child understand his moods and learn to read simple words at the same time. Make several cards with simple sentences printed on them . . . I feel happy, I feel sleepy, or I feel angry. Attach a piece of string to each end of the card so that your child can wear them around his neck. Let him suggest other words or phrases to print on cards.

Yes or No?

Make two cards, one with "yes" printed on it and the other with "no." Ask your child some questions and have her answer by flashing the appropriate card.

Newspaper Search

The newspaper is a great teaching tool for children. Let your child see how many words he can identify on a page. He will probably do quite well in the advertisement section and can read names of products he is familiar with.

14

writing stories and making books

Command Cards

Make a variety of cards with simple commands printed on them. Your child will have fun reading the cards and following the printed commands. At first the commands can be very easy, perhaps only one word like hop, sing, jump, smile or laugh. Later on you can make the words more difficult, such as walk to the door, look out the window, or clean up your room!

Making New Words

Give your child some examples of compound words . . . like sidewalk, butterfly, necktie, bedroom, cowboy, carport, or hairbrush. See if the two of you can dream up some more.

First, Middle, Last

To help your child understand that most people have a first, middle and last name, write her name using three separate cards. She can then practice putting her name in the proper order. Do the same with the names of other members of the family.

Dictation

One way to increase your child's interest in words and speaking is to let him dictate stories to you. He will be delighted to see you write down his thoughts. Why not make a book out of some of his ideas. He can illustrate and you can write the story down for him on the opposite page. Don't worry about grammar or improper word usage. The most important thing is to give your child the confidence to express himself freely. When he begins to write words, he will want to write the captions for his illustrations himself.

Binding Books

There are several ways to bind your child's books. You can simply staple the edges together or lace them together with yarn. Covers can be made from fabric scraps, wrapping paper, contact paper or wallpaper. If you want to preserve a particular book for a long time, you might want to make a cover out of cardboard or buy an inexpensive notebook binder.

Books, Books, Books

Encourage your child to make books on things that interest him (even if the subject doesn't appeal to you). You might suggest a *Touch Me Book* that has material of different textures pasted in it, an *Alphabet Book*, a *Shapes Book* or a *Poetry Book* with illustrations of his favorite poems. Also experiment making them different shapes and sizes.

classification and matching

Wallpaper Match

Mount a large piece of wallpaper on cardboard. Cut a duplicate piece of wallpaper into sections which will match the large section of wallpaper. Let your child practice matching the wallpaper pattern pieces by laying each piece on top of its corresponding pattern. The small pieces can be stored in a large envelope.

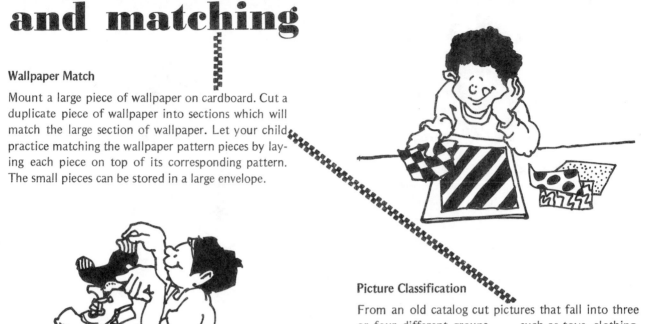

Things That Go Together

From an old catalog or magazine cut out pictures of things that usually go together . . . like shoes and socks, wallet and money, lamp and lampshade or cup and saucer. Scatter these pictures on the floor and let your child try to match the pictures of things that go together.

Touch and Match

Collect two each of a variety of items . . . 2 spoons, 2 jar lids, 2 pencils or 2 pieces of sand paper. Put one set of the items in a paper bag. Hand your child the others one at a time. Have him reach into the bag, feel around and try to find the match. No peeking!

Color Match

Cut a large circle out of cardboard. Divide it into eight sections and cover each with a different color of paper. Paint clothespins to match the colors on the circle. Your child can match the colors by clipping the clothespins to their corresponding colors.

Picture Classification

From an old catalog cut pictures that fall into three or four different groups . . . such as toys, clothing, furniture, pets, fruits, vegetables or transportation. You can glue these pictures onto pieces of cardboard to make them last longer. Let your child practice sorting them into appropriate piles.

Button Sort

Glue different styles of buttons to the bottom of each section of an egg carton. Place other matching buttons in a small container. Your child can sort these buttons by putting them into the appropriate sections of the egg carton.

skills that improve writing coordination

The most important thing that you can do to help your child build coordination for writing is to provide her with ample opportunity to use her muscles, both large and small. That means a lot of running, climbing, throwing, swinging, dancing, cutting, scribbling, painting and pasting. It is only after your child has developed these muscles that she will be able to coordinate her eye and hand movements to perform the difficult task of writing letters and numbers.

Tracing

Let your child trace a picture through very thin paper or trace around blocks and objects of various shapes and sizes.

Nuts and Bolts

Gather an assortment of nuts and bolts of different sizes. Mix them up in a container. Children delight in finding the corresponding sizes and screwing the nuts and bolts together. For very young children, use large nuts and bolts and limit the quantity.

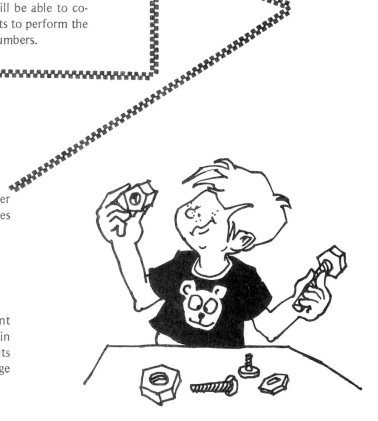

Touch the Snake

Children often write their names from right to left when they first experiment with pencil and paper. To help your child improve his left to right orientation, place a squiggly snakelike line along the left-hand edge of a piece of paper. Have your child begin each line of writing by touching the snake and then "running away" by writing toward the right.

getting ready to read and write〜〜〜〜〜

For the adult:

Burie, Audrey Ann. *Reading With a Smile* (Washington, D.C.: Acropolis, 1975). Child-centered activities for home or school.

Chall, J.S. *Learning To Read: The Great Debate* (New York: McGraw-Hill, 1967). A critical evaluation of instructional methods.

Cromwell, Ellen. *Feathers In My Cap: Early Reading Through Experience* (Washington, D.C.: Acropolis, 1980). Combines the learning experience approach with phonics.

Heater, S.H. *Teaching Preschool Reading* (Provo, Utah: Brigham Young University Press, 1980). Provides prereading enrichment ideas as well as suggestions for actual reading instruction.

Hymes, James. *Before the Child Reads* (New York: Harper & Row, 1964).

Kirchner, Audrey. *Basic Beginnings: Learning Games and Activities For Young Children* (Washington, D.C.: Acropolis, 1980). More than 100 learning activities, games, lesson plans and ready-to-use patterns.

Larrick, Nancy. *A Parent's Guide To Children's Reading* (New York: Bantam, 1975). Updated and revised edition of this classic reference for selecting reading material for children of all ages and every reading level.

Lee, D.M., and Allen, R.V. *Learning To Read Through Experience* (New York: Appleton-Century-Crofts, 1963). Using the child's own experience as the starting point for building a relevant, meaningful reading vocabulary.

Peterson, Rosemary. *Handbook For Teaching Beginning Reading Skills in Early Childhood Education* (Moraga, Calif: St. Mary's College, 1976). Excellent guide for sequence of reading skills instruction.

Pfaum, Susanna. *The Development Of Language and Reading In Young Children* (Columbus, Ohio: Charles E. Merrill, 1974). Practical ideas for developing language skills at home or in the classroom.

Smethurst, Wood. *Teaching Your Child To Read At Home* (New York: McGraw-Hill, 1976). A review of the most recent research on teaching reading to preschoolers as well as suggestions for actual reading instruction.

Teale, W.H. *Early Reading: An Annotated Bibliography* (New York: International Reading Association, 1980).

For the child:

Aardema, Berna. *Why Mosquitoes Buzz In People's Ears* (Dial, 1978).

Carle, Eric. *All About Arthur* (Franklin-Watts, 1974).

Charlip, Remy. *Mother, Mother, I Feel Sick* (Parents' Magazine Press, 1973).

Feelings, Muriel. *Jambo Means Hello: Swahili Alphabet Book* (Dial, 1974).

Goff, Beth. *Where Is Daddy? The Story Of a Divorce* (Beacon, 1973).

Keats, Ezra Jack. *Goggles* (Macmillan, 1969).

McCloskey, Robert. *Make Way For Ducklings* (Viking, 1941).

Rey, H.A. *Curious George Learns the Alphabet* (Houghton Mifflin, 1963).

Sendak, Maurice. *Where the Wild Things Are* (Harper & Row, 1974).

Silverstein, Shel. *Giving Tree* (Harper & Row, 1964).

Silverstein, Shel. *Where the Sidewalk Ends* (Harper & Row, 1974).

Viorst, Judith. *Alexander and the Terrible, Horrible, No Good, Very Bad Day* (Atheneum, 1976).

Zion, Gene. *Harry the Dirty Dog* (Harper, 1956).

Zolotow, Charlotte. *William's Doll* (Harper & Row, 1972).

learning math concepts

There are endless opportunities to help your child when s/he is first learning math concepts. The activities you provide at home are essential for instilling the skills s/he will need throughout life. When you work with your child, however, keep in mind that s/he will understand math concepts better if s/he works directly with concrete objects. In other words, if your child is learning to count, make sure that all the objects s/he is counting are physically present. Whether s/he is counting the napkins on the dinner table, the pillows on the sofa or the buttons on a shirt, have your child touch each object as s/he says the appropriate number. Also remember that children build on what they already know; so use every opportunity possible to review what s/he has learned previously. S/he will be far more willing to try a hand at more difficult tasks is s/he has been successful many times with activities s/he has already mastered.

using numbers and counting things

Footprints

Trace around your child's foot on ten pieces of cardboard. Cut out the footprints. Number them from 1-10. Have him arrange them in order and practice counting while he walks, or mix them up and call out different numbers for him to jump on.

Number Cards

With a felt-tipped marker or black crayon, make large numbers (0-10) on pieces of cardboard that are approximately 15 cm x 22 cm (6" x 9"). Your child can practice arranging her number cards in the proper sequence. Keep in mind, however, that understanding number concepts means far more than being able to count to a high number or arrange numbers in their proper order. To help your child understand that numbers are associated with different quantities, you might want to give her a box full of objects (1 pinecone, 2 buttons, 3 clothespins, 4 spoons, 5 paperclips . . . and so on) and let her arrange the objects next to the appropriate card.

Numbers, Numbers Everywhere

Find them . . . on the TV dial, on license plates, on a typewriter, on the telephone, on your house, in the newspaper, on price tags, on the clock, at the grocery store, in the telephone book, on a deck of cards or on speed limit signs.

What Doesn't Belong?

Use a deck of playing cards. Arrange four cards, three of the same number and one that doesn't belong. Your child can pick out the one that is different.

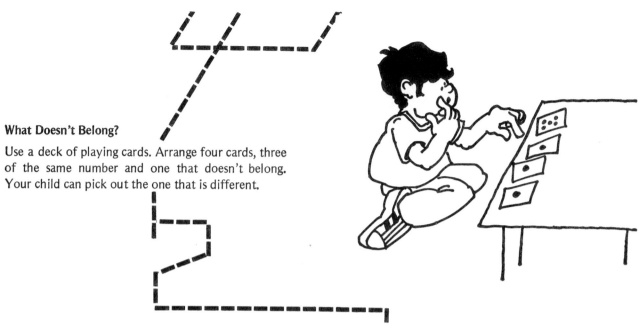

Button Count

Number the compartments of a muffin tin from 0-11. Provide your child with 66 buttons. Let him place the correct number of buttons in each compartment. If he is correct, all the buttons will be used up.

Take a Survey

Take a survey of your home. Count and write down how many chairs, windows, pillows, pictures and toothbrushes you have. Let your child think of other things to count and record.

What Is Zero?

You will probably have to explain the concept of zero to your child. One way to do this is to give examples and let her make up her own. For instance, "There are zero elephants in the refrigerator" or "There are zero firetrucks in the garage." Include zero in your games whenever possible.

size

Scrambled Lids

Make a collection of many different sized jars. Save the lids. Put them all in a box and let your child figure out which lid fits which jar.

Large and Small

On a table place several pairs of different objects that are the same except for size. For example, a large plate and a small one, a large sponge and a small sponge, a large spoon and a small one, or use glasses, balls, scissors, records or books. Have your child sort them according to size, putting all the large objects on one half of the table and all the smaller ones on the other half of the table.

What Is Large?

Ask your child to find something that is . . . larger than a peanut but smaller than a pear . . . larger than a pencil but smaller than a telephone pole . . . larger than a cat but smaller than a kangaroo. Think of others.

ordering

The Line Up

Collect four to six bottles of the same type (syrup or soda bottles are good). Fill up the bottles with different amounts of colored water, leaving one bottle completely empty. Seal all the bottles. Your child can practice putting the bottles in order from the least to the most.

Short to Long

Cut up several drinking straws so they are different lengths. Have your child arrange them in order from shortest to longest. Begin with only three straw lengths and gradually increase the number as your child masters each level of difficulty. You might also want to use cardboard tubes like those used for paper towels or toilet paper; however, these are more difficult to cut.

shape

Shape a Rope

Make large shapes on the floor with an old rope or clothesline. You might want to give your child directions to follow using whatever shape he has just made . . . jump in and out of the circle . . . put one leg in the triangle and the other leg out . . . sit in the square.

Circle Puzzle

Cut several large circles from cardboard or heavy paper. Then cut the circle into two or three parts making an interesting pattern along the cut edge. Let your child practice putting the pieces together.

Find It

Look inside or outside your house for different shapes.

Round: buttons, spools, clocks, bottlecaps, coins, dishes, doorknobs, jars, wheels, records.

Square: matchbooks, bolts, dice, windowpanes, postage stamps, sugar cubes.

Triangle: TV antenna, earrings, a sailboat sail, "Yield" signs, rooftops.

Rectangle: doors, tables, books, piano seats, baking pans, a bathroom mirror, cereal boxes.

Make a Shape

Cut an assortment of traingles from cardboard or heavy paper. Vary the sizes of the triangles so that when fit together they will make a larger triangle or another geometric shape. Let your child have fun arranging them into interesting patterns and shapes. More durable shapes can be cut from balsa wood or from very thin plywood.

Stretch-It Board

Pound ten to fifteen nails in a random pattern half way into a board that is approximately 23 cm x 30 cm (9" x 12"). Let your child practice making interesting shapes by stretching colored rubber bands around the nails.

23

measuring, weighing and balancing things

Weigh and Record

Using the bathroom scale, weigh and record how many kilograms your child weighs. Then let her think of other things to weigh . . . like you.

Make a Scale

Cut off the bottom section of a hanger. Attach three strings to each end. These strings can be stapled or tied to two balancing dishes made from pie tins or plastic coffee can lids. Hang the hooked section of the hanger on a door knob or railing so that it can swing freely. Weigh and balance different things: three pencils and two pinecones, four acorns and one clothespin. Let your child think of other things to balance and weigh.

Balancing Blocks

Lay a board that is about 60 cm (2 feet) long and 10 cm (4") wide on top of a fulcrum 8 cm (3" dowel cut in half). Mark the board into different units and let your child practice balancing smaller blocks on it.

How Long?

Let your child experiment measuring things with a meter stick. It doesn't matter how accurate he is at first. What is important is that he is beginning to use comparison words like longer, shorter, wider and narrower.

Help your child think of imaginative ways to measure different things around the house. For example, "the book is five hands long," "the dog is ten pencils long," "the foot is twenty pennies long."

After repeated experiences in measuring in this informal way, your child will begin to see the need for standard units of measurement. Only then will words like centimeter, decimeter and meter have any relevance.

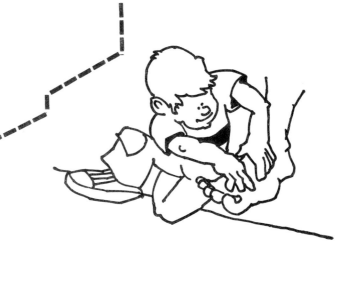

time

How Long Does It Take?

Using a timer or the minute hand on a clock, let your child see how long it takes him to get dressed, brush his teeth or watch a program on television.

What Is a Minute?

Let your child guess how many times she can touch her toes in one minute, how many cars will pass the house in one minute or how many crackers she can eat in one minute. Then check. Let her think of other guessing games that will instill the concept of one minute.

Paper Plate Clock

Help your child make the numbers from 1-12 around the edge of a paper plate so that the plate resembles a clock. With a brad, attach two hands in the center of the clock. Set the clock to show your child what time Sesame Street comes on, what time dinner will be ready or what time he goes to bed. To help him become familiar with "time" words, use them often. For instance: "We will eat in fifteen minutes," "The show begins at two o'clock," or "The cookies will take one half an hour to bake."

learning math concepts ------------

For the adult:

Burns, Marilyn, *I Hate Mathematics! Book* (Boston: Little & Brown, 1975). Imaginative, fun ways to instill important mathematical concepts in children. Geared primarily for elementary-age children but can be simplified for preschoolers also.

Copeland, Richard, *How Children Learn Mathematics* (New York: Macmillan, 1974). Implications of Piaget's theory to instruction of mathematical concepts in early childhood education as well as the elementary and junior high school levels.

Hirsch, Elisabeth, *The Block Book* (Washington, D.C.: National Association for the Education of Young Children, 1974). The importance of block play for instilling important math concepts.

Piaget, Jean, *The Psychology of the Child* (New York: Basic Books, 1969). Definitive presentation of the development of logico-mathematical concepts in young children.

Sharp, Evelyn, *Thinking Is Child's Play* (New York: Avon, 1969). Homemade games and activities for math.

U.S. Department of Commerce, *What About Metric?* (Washington, D.C.: Superintendent of Documents, # 030-01191). Simple introduction to thinking metric.

For the child:

Carle, Eric. *My Very First Book of Numbers* (Crowell, 1974).

Carle, Eric. *My Very First Book of Shapes* (Crowell, 1974).

Children's Television Workshop. *Seasame Street Book of Numbers* (Preschool Press, Time-Life).

Langstaff, John. *Over in the Meadow* (Harcourt, Brace & Co., 1967).

LeSieg, Theo. *Ten Apples Up On Top* (Random House, Beginner Books, 1961).

Lionni, Leo. *Biggest House In The World* (Pantheon, 1968).

Dr. Seuss. *500 Hats of Bartholomew Cubbins* (Hale, 1938).

Silverstein, Shel. *A Giraffe and a Half* (Harper & Row, 1974).

Untermeyer, Louis. *One & One & One* (Crowell & Collier, 1965).

Wildsmith, Brian. *Brian Wildsmith's 1, 2, 3's* (Franklin Watts, 1970).

Zim, Herbert. *Metric Measure* (Morrow, 1974).

Ziner, Feenie. *Counting Carnival* (Coward-McCann, 1970).

discovery through science

The inquisitive nature of children makes them natural scientists. They continually search to find out the how, why, what and where of things around them. Encourage this kind of questioning and exploring. Give your child as many opportunities as possible to investigate, examine and experiment. By piecing together bits and pieces of information, s/he will gradually begin to understand some of the puzzling and intriguing aspects of the world in which s/he lives.

plants and seeds

Watch It Sprout

Stick two or three toothpicks into the top portion of a carrot. Lay the toothpicks on the rim of a small glass or container of water so that the bottom of the carrot is in the water. Watch it sprout and grow in a few days. Also try growing beets, radishes, onions and turnips in the same way.

Seeds and Pits

Let your child make a collection of different kinds of seeds and pits like those from an orange, a watermelon, grapes, a sunflower or a peach. He might also enjoy growing some seeds and pits like those from a pumpkin, apple, dates, prunes or an avocado. Place the seeds in water in a sunny spot and be very patient. Eventually they will split and begin to sprout. At that point you can either plant them in soil or leave them in water.

The Long Journey

To help your child understand how plants get their food, explain that inside a plant there are many roads that the food travels on to get to the top of the plant. These roads are called veins. The food from the ground (water and minerals) travels up the plant's roots into the veins and feeds the plant. You might want to get a large leaf and point out the veins on the leaf. You might also want to do the following experiment. Put a celery stalk into a glass of colored water. Watch the leaves turn the color of the water in a few hours. Cut across the stalk and point out the veins to your child.

Sweet Potato Plant

Stick three or four toothpicks around the middle of a sweet potato or yam. Place it in a container of water so the toothpicks support the potato on the rim of the container. Place in some sunlight and replenish water when it gets to a low level. In several weeks it will sprout into a beautiful plant.

Rub a Tree

Next time you go to the park with your child, take along several pieces of paper and some crayons that have had the paper removed. Select a tree and feel the bark. Talk about how the bark feels to touch. Now place the paper on the bark and rub gently with the side of the crayon until the bark's contour begins to show up on the paper. If you try several kinds of trees, you'll see different bark patterns emerge. This paper might make an interesting gift wrapping paper, too.

Sponge Grass

Put a sponge in a small saucer of water to keep it moist. Sprinkle some grass seed on top of the sponge . . . and in a few days . . . Presto!

Or you and your child can make a furry cucumber by poking holes all over a cucumber and filling them with grass seed or wheat berries. Attach a string and hang. No need to water . . . sprouts should appear in a few days.

Mother Nature Preserves

The next time you take a nature walk with your child, select a few dried specimens like wild oats, thistles, twigs and grasses. Then round up an empty jar and put a small piece of clay or play dough in the lid of the jar. Now make a simple arrangement of the dried specimens standing up in the clay. Carefully place the jar over the display and screw on the cap so that the jar will rest upside down. Beautiful!

Tube and Tape Nature Collage

Another way to preserve some outdoor specimens is to take two long cardboard tubes like those from paper towels and secure pieces of masking tape between the two so that it looks like an opened scroll. Now your child can place the feathers, sticks, twigs and dried grasses she collected on the sticky tape. Press so that they hold securely and hang.

By the Skin of Our Onion??

Dyeing eggs with natural dyes can be lots of fun and the results can be spectacular. Here's how:

Place about eight layers of onion skins in the toe of an old stocking. Put bits of rice, leaves, flower petals and grasses on top of the skins. Place an egg on top of the material and wrap carefully. Secure with string and place in a pot of water and boil for 30 minutes. Cool and untie the stocking . . . Wow!

That Fuzzy Stuff Called Mold

Leave a piece of bread out overnight. The following day place it in a closed jar and put the jar in a damp warm place. Watch the mold grow in a few days. Mold is also fascinating to look at with a magnifying glass.

air

What Is It?

Explain to your child that we can't see air or taste it but we still know that it's there. To help her understand, take her outside to watch a tree, a kite or a flag blow in the wind. Use an air pump to inflate a bicycle tire or let her blow up a balloon. You might also want to try the following experiment. Place a napkin in the bottom of a glass. Place the glass upside down into a bowl of water. Let your child see how the glass does not fill up with water and the napkin stays dry. Now tilt the glass so that bubbles rise to the surface of the water. What happens?

What Is a Bubble? Make Some.

Mix together in a baby jar 60 ml (¼ cup) liquid dish detergent, 120 ml (½ cup) water, and a few drops of food coloring. You might also add 5 ml (1 tsp.) of glycerine to make the bubbles longlasting. Glycerine can be purchased at most hardware stores. Provide your child with a plastic straw or twist a wire to make a bubble blower. Great fun!

The Magic of Yeast

Mix a packet of yeast in a glass of warm water. Put a rubber glove over the top of the glass and watch the glove inflate as the yeast is activated . . . . One thing leads to another . . . . Why not try out this yeast magic on your favorite bread recipe? Your child will delight in watching the dough rise . . . and punching it down again, too.

Up, Up and Away . . .

A hot air balloon isn't the only means of traveling through the sky. Look through several magazines with your child and cut out pictures of other things that fly . .

like birds, airplanes, rocketships and glider planes. These pictures can then be glued on a big piece of paper cut in the shape of a diamond. Now your child will have a kite to fly on a breezy day.

Why not extend this activity into a land, water, air game? Collect different pictures for each category and mix them up. Your child will have fun sorting them into different piles according to their category.

magnets and magnifying glasses

Magnifying Magic

Next time your child's birthday comes around, buy him a magnifying glass. You'll be amazed at the hours of entertainment he'll derive from this educational toy. Let him examine a piece of skin, a penny, some pond water, a nylon stocking or an insect. Here are a few experiments that are especially exciting to observe with a magnifying glass.

— Put about 45 ml (3 tbsps.) of baking soda in a small jar. Add a small amount of vinegar. Stir and watch what happens.

— Put an egg white in a small jar of water. Observe the change over a few days.

Make It Move

Float several metal bottle caps in a bowl of water. By holding a magnet near the caps (but not touching them) your child can move the bottle caps wherever she directs them. She can also scatter thumb tacks on a piece of cardboard. While you support the cardboard, she can move the magnet underneath to make the thumbtacks move on top.

Pick Up

Collect a variety of different objects like a rubber band, paper clip, penny, hairpin, safety pin, thumbtack, straight pin or a jar lid. Ask your child to guess which objects the magnet will pick up; then she can experiment with the magnet to see if her guesses were correct.

machines

Machine Hunt

Take a walk around your house with your child and look for as many different kinds of machines as you can find . . . like a pencil sharpener, egg beater, can opener, record player, typewriter, clock or a vacuum cleaner. Also look for simple machines like a pair of scissors or a hole puncher.

Pinch Up

Provide your child with a pair of tongs, a clothespin and some tweezers. Have him practice picking things up with them to help him understand what these simple machines have in common.

Don't Throw It Away

The next time an old clock, egg timer or wrist watch breaks, don't throw it away. Give it to your child and let her take it apart and play with it.

water

Swirling Waves

Fill an empty bottle about 3/4 full with water. Add food coloring until the water is a deep color. Now add mineral oil or vegetable oil until the bottle is completely full. Cap securely. Your child will be amazed to watch the swirling motion of the waves he creates by gently rocking the bottle back and forth.

Evaporation

Place a jar of water in the sun. Mark the water level on the side of the jar with a black crayon or felt-tipped marker. Observe what happens to the water after a few hours, a day or two days.

Water Is Water, Or Is It?

The next time it rains, let your child put a bowl outside to catch some rain water. Fill up another bowl with regular faucet water. Get two handkerchiefs and dip one into the rain water and the other into a bowl of faucet water. Let them dry. Compare how the handkerchiefs feel. Then let your child stir a capful of dishsoap into each bowl and compare how the two types of water make suds.

Making Rainbows

Adjust a hose to make a fine spray. Stand with your back to the sun and watch the rainbow of colors in the water spray.

Sink Or Float?

Collect a variety of different objects like a cork, penny, bottle cap, pencil, paperclip, ping pong ball, rubber band or a piece of soap. Let your child guess whether each of these things will sink or float. Give her a bowl of water and let her test whether or not her guess was correct. She might also enjoy making a walnut boat to float. Put a small piece of play dough into the hollow of a walnut half. Put a toothpick through a triangular piece of paper and secure it in the play dough. Then float it. Make a whole fleet of walnut boats and sail them in the bath tub.

Dripping Droplets

Provide your child with a small jar of plain water, an eye dropper and a tray with the following items on it: a small sponge, a few cotton balls, a small piece of material and small samples of foil, plastic wrap, writing paper, a paper towel and waxed paper. He will enjoy experimenting with dripping droplets onto the different surfaces. A truly absorbing activity?!

Kaleidoscope of Colors

Fill a white styrofoam egg carton one half full of water. Give your child three small jars of colored water (blue, yellow and red) along with three eye droppers. She will love to experiment with mixing these primary colors together in different combinations in the egg carton holes to create an array of secondary colors. A wonderful follow-up activity would be to read the story of *Little Yellow, Little Blue* by Leo Lionni.

Making Rain

Fill a small pan with ice and hold it over a boiling kettle. Let your child observe what happens when the hot steam hits the bottom of the small pan.

Soap Crayons

A sure way to get a reluctant preschooler in the bathtub for a scrub. Mix approximately 40 ml (1/6 cup) of water with 240 ml (1 cup) soap flakes. Add food coloring to desired color. Press this mixture into a mold like an ice cube tray or a popsicle mold. Let it dry for a couple of days until hard and firm. Remove and let your child have fun scribbling on the tub during bath time.

light

Spot It

Let your child place a small mirror in a glass of water. Adjust the glass until the sun shines on the mirror. The mirror should reflect a rainbow of colors against the wall or ceiling. He might also want to hold the mirror in his hands while standing in the sun and make the spot of light bounce around the room. Spot it and catch it.

Leaf Prints

Collect an assortment of interesting leaves. Place them on a piece of colored paper out in the sun for a few hours. Remove the leaves and see what the sunlight has created on the paper.

The Broken Pencil

Put a pencil in a glass of water. Let your child look at it from the side of the glass. The refraction of light will cause it to look broken.

Shadow Play

Hang a sheet across a doorway. Put a light behind the sheet and let your child have fun creating different shadows while he stands between the light and the sheet. If you sit in front of the sheet you can watch the performance. Shadows are also fun to watch (and try to catch) outside. Take your child outside at different times on a sunny day to compare the length of the shadows his body makes.

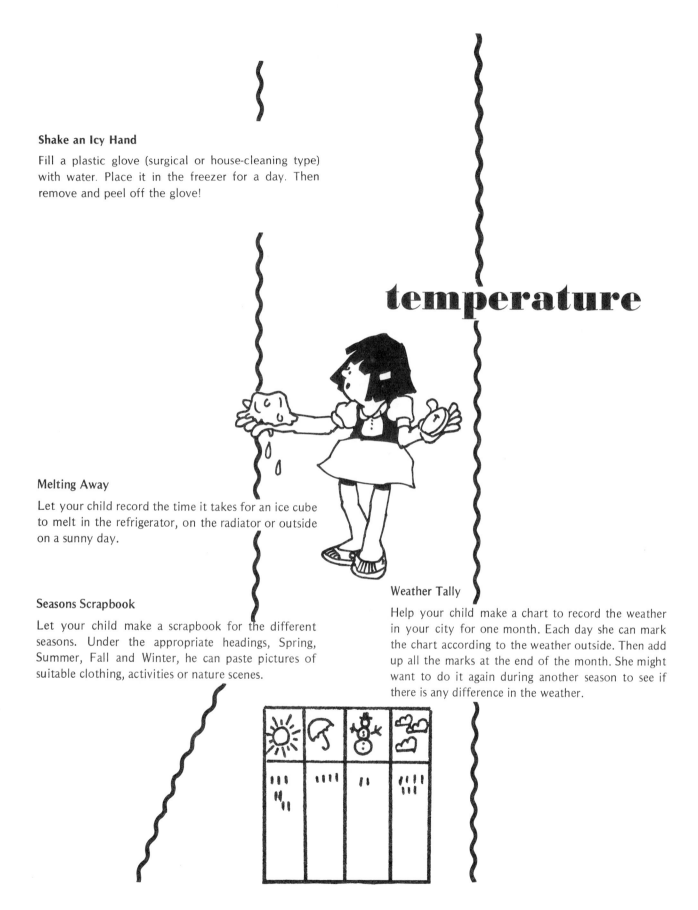

Shake an Icy Hand

Fill a plastic glove (surgical or house-cleaning type) with water. Place it in the freezer for a day. Then remove and peel off the glove!

temperature

Melting Away

Let your child record the time it takes for an ice cube to melt in the refrigerator, on the radiator or outside on a sunny day.

Seasons Scrapbook

Let your child make a scrapbook for the different seasons. Under the appropriate headings, Spring, Summer, Fall and Winter, he can paste pictures of suitable clothing, activities or nature scenes.

Weather Tally

Help your child make a chart to record the weather in your city for one month. Each day she can mark the chart according to the weather outside. Then add up all the marks at the end of the month. She might want to do it again during another season to see if there is any difference in the weather.

discovery through science～～～

For the adult:

Cobb, Vicki. *Science Experiments You Can Eat* (New York: Lippincott, 1972). The activities in this handbook are geared primarily for older children, but with a little extra guidance, they can be adapted for preschoolers.

Cornell, Joseph. *Sharing Nature With Children* (Nevada City, Calif.: Ananda Publications, 1979). Suggestions on how to be an effective nature guide with young children.

Euston, Carol. *A Better Place To Be: A Guide to Environmental Learning* (Washington, D.C.: Government Printing Office, Document #2400-00805). A good guide for instilling environmental awareness in children.

Fiarotta, Phyllis. *Snips and Snails and Walnut Whales* (New York: Workman Publishing, 1975). Nature crafts by the dozens.

Frankel, Lillian, and Frankel, Godfrey. *101 Best Nature Games and Projects* (New York: Gramercy Publishing Co., 1959). Good for older children, too.

Gjersvik, Maryanne. *Green Fun* (Riverside, Conn.: Chatham Press, 1974). Imaginative outdoor projects.

Holt, Bess-Gene. *Science With Young Children* (Washington, D.C.: National Association for the Education of Young Children, 1977). Rationales, methods and materials for teachers to help children discover important concepts in science.

Nickelsburg, Janet. *Nature Activities For Early Childhood* (Reading, Mass.: Addison-Wesley, 1976). A science teacher of 48 years shares her collection of outdoor and indoor natural science activities.

Petrich, Patricia. *The Kids' Garden Book* (Concord, Calif.: Nitty Gritty Publications, 1974). Guaranteed to turn your thumb green.

Russell, Helen Ross. *Ten-Minute Field Trips* (Chicago: J.G. Ferguson, 1973). An indispensable resource guide for anyone interested in environmental education.

Skelsey, Alice. *Growing Up Green* (New York: Workman Publishing, 1973). Activities for parents and children gardening together.

For the child:

Bendick, Jeanne. *Living Things* (Franklin-Watts, 1969).
Branley, Franklin M. *Mickey's Magnet* (Crowell, 1956).
Dunn, Judy. *Animal Friends* (Creative Education, 1970).
Freeman, Mae and Ira. *You Will Go To the Moon* (Random House, 1971).
Krauss, Ruth. *The Carrot Seed* (Harper & Row, 1945).
Fujikawa, Gyo. *Let's Grow a Garden* (Grossett & Dunlap, 1978).
Wildsmith, Brian. *Animal Homes* (Oxford University Press, 1980).
Zolotow, Charlotte. *The Storm Book* (Harper & Row, 1952).

Excellent science book series:

Books For Young Explorers (National Geographic).
Let's Find Out Science Books (Franklin Watts).
Living Science Books (Grossett & Dunlap).
True Book Series (Children's Press).

Two excellent monthly science publications for young children:
Ranger Rick's Nature Magazine available from National Wildlife Federation, 1412 16th Street N.W., Washington, D.C. 20036.
World Magazine available from National Geographic Society, 17th & M Streets N.W., Washington, D.C. 20036.

creating through art and music

Art and music are nonverbal ways children communicate ideas and feelings about the world. In this type of communication, it is the process of creating that should be stressed and not the final product. In other words, the sensations and enjoyment children experience when they paint are far more important than the final pictures they produce. Similarly, in music it is the way children feel and respond to rhythm and grow in their appreciation of a wide range of musical selections that should be encouraged and not necessarily how precisely they can duplicate tone, pitch and rhythm.

The activities in this section will help stretch the child's imagination and express his or her unique individuality. When doing an art project, try to give children as few instructions as possible. Avoid comparing and judging and resist showing them how to draw a particular object. Copying what you have done defeats the whole purpose of the activity because it encourages children to depend on you as a model. Their artistic competence and creativity will unfold naturally if they are allowed to develop at their own rate. So be patient and provide ample opportunities to explore new modes of expression. Encourage creative endeavors by displaying their art work and talking to them about what they have done.

painting

Easel Paint Recipe

To get the most for your money, buy dry tempera powder. Each time you need paint, you can mix a small amount of the powder with water. The paint consistency should be like thick cream. Adding a little detergent will make the paint wash out more easily. You might also try adding a small amount of liquid starch or baby oil to the mixed paint for an interesting effect. Start your child with the primary colors first (red, blue and yellow). Later he can practice mixing these colors in different combinations to produce green, orange and purple. He can paint on old paper bags, butcher paper, old gift wrapping paper or plain newsprint (from your newspaper).

Improvise

Your child can produce imaginative works of art *without* paint brushes. She can dip a string into a container of paint and swirl it on a piece of paper or make a creepy spider picture by blowing a blotch of paint around on a piece of paper with an ordinary drinking straw. She can also produce interesting pictures with Q-tips, an old toothbrush, an eye dropper, an old bottle brush or a roll-on deodorant bottle that has been filled with paint.

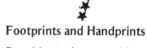

Footprints and Handprints

Do this project outside on a sunny day. Let your child paint his hands and feet with easel paint, then quickly print on a piece of large paper. You might also place the paint in a shallow pan so he can step into it and then hop around on the paper.

Shine-Through Painting

Spread some salad oil over a picture your child has just painted. When you hang it in a window, the light will shine through.

Soap Snow

Whip about 480 ml (2 cups) soap flakes with 120 ml (½ cup) of water to the consistency of whipped cream. Put on paper to use as fingerpaint or in a pastry tube to be squeezed out into a design.

Drip and Squish

Let your child drip some paint on one half of a piece of paper. Fold over the other half and press. Open up.

Crayon Painting

Melt crayon scraps in a muffin pan over boiling water. Using a brush, your child can paint designs onto an old sheet, apron, cloth napkin, shirt or smock. Iron the material and the colors will stay in permanently.

Printing

Cut an orange, lemon, potato, carrot or pear into a variety of interesting shapes. Let your child dip these items into a shallow dish of paint and then press them on a piece of paper. You can suggest that she make the printing object "hop like a bunny" across the piece of paper so the paint won't smear. Let her experiment printing with other gadgets around the house . . . like hair curlers, sponges, nuts and bolts, kitchen utensils, bottle caps, clothespins, cookie cutters, or crumpled paper. Be prepared for a mess.

crayons, scissors, paper and paste

Paste Recipe

Mix 240 ml (1 cup) flour with 240 ml cold water. Add to 800 ml (3¼ cups) boiling water. Cook until the mixture is clear. Add 5 ml (1 tsp.) alum as a preservative. Store in tightly covered jars.

Glue Tip

Some of the art projects in this section call for glue instead of paste. You will save money in the long run if you buy a large container of Elmers at a discount hardware store. Then stretch your investment by mixing 15 ml (1 tbsp.) glue with 30 ml (2 tbsp.) water each time your child needs some glue.

Paper Is Paper, Or Is It?

Don't limit your child's artistic endeavors to plain white paper. Let him experiment coloring on as many different kinds as possible . . . like sandpaper, butcher paper, paper towels, graph paper, paper napkins, the want ads section from a newspaper, wallpaper scraps, toilet paper, cardboard, paper bags, freezer paper (try both sides), adding machine paper, discarded computer print-out paper or paper cut into different shapes. If you have any carbon paper around, give your child a piece or two to experiment with. He'll think it's magic to see his artistic creations come out in duplicate or triplicate.

  Also, raid the trash basket at your local picture framing store. These art stores often discard pieces of matting that are ideal for art projects.

Peel Off

Peel off the paper around a few of your child's crayons. Put notches or grooves in them and let your child color by rubbing the crayons on their side onto a piece of paper.

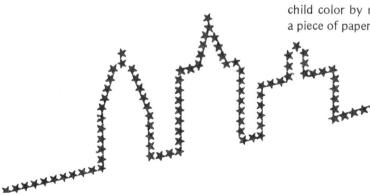

Eraser Picture

Cover a piece of paper with pencil marks using the side of the lead. Your child can then "draw" a picture by erasing away the lead into whatever design he wants.

Color Press

Using an ordinary kitchen grater, help your child grate old crayons into many small shavings. Arrange these shavings on a piece of waxed paper. Cover with another piece of waxed paper the same size. Press with a hot iron . . . Wow!

Box People

Collect several cardboard boxes of different shapes and sizes. Help your child construct box people by taping the boxes together and paint on appropriate features. Yarn, steel wool or Easter grass can be glued on for hair. She might also want to glue on empty spools for the eyes and a bottle cap for the nose.

Crayon Resist

Your child can make a crayon resist by pressing very hard with the crayons while she makes a design on a piece of heavy paper. Then paint over the entire picture with thin black or purple paint and watch the crayon design show through.

Patchwork Picture

Cut out an assortment of different material scraps. Let your child patch a picture together by gluing the material scraps onto a piece of heavy paper or cardboard.

Paper Towel Design

Fold a piece of paper towel several times. Dip the corners of the towel into different colors of food coloring mixed in water. Unfold the towel and spread out to dry.

litterbug art

Collages

Interesting collages can be made from many things you would ordinarily throw away. Simply provide your child with a variety of litterbug materials and some paste or glue; her imagination will carry on from there. Things to save: bottle caps, steel wool pads, toothpicks, string, rubber bands, old ribbons, burned out flash bulbs, popsicle sticks, used gift wrapping paper, old sponges, sawdust, jar lids, bark, nut shells, cupcake or candy papers, material scraps, pebbles, acorns, nuts, bolts, washers, old jewelry, tinsel, buttons, magazine pictures, comics from the Sunday newspaper, old buckles, shoelaces, broken zippers, styrofoam packing, Easter grass, straws, tile or scraps of linoleum, rug scraps, old golf tees, pebbles or feathers.

Newspaper Animals

Don't throw away those old newspapers; save them to make a whole collection of stuffed animals. Put four large pieces on top of one another. With a crayon, draw the shape of an animal such as a turtle or a fish on the top piece. Keeping all four pieces together, have your child cut out the animal shape. Staple along the edges except for a small opening. Stuff with wads of newspaper. Each side of the animal should be two pieces thick. Staple closed and paint.

Making Blocks

Instead of throwing away used milk cartons, make blocks out of them for your child. Wash out the insides of two cartons and cut off the top sections. Then fit one carton inside the other. Tape closed. Let your child paint them different colors and designs. If you add a small amount of detergent to the paint it will adhere to the waxy surface of the cartons. Another way to make blocks is to cut old lumber scraps into different shapes and sizes and sand until smooth.

sculpturing

Soap Sculptures

Leave a bar of Ivory Soap unwrapped for 24 hours. Give your child a small dull kitchen knife and let him chip away at the soap.

Wire Sculptures

The next time the telephone man installs a telephone in your neighborhood, ask him for extra pieces of colored telephone wire. They're great fun to twist and turn and make sculptures out of.

Ice Sculptures

Wash out a large milk carton and fill with water. Freeze. Peel off the carton. Provide your child with a screwdriver and a small hammer and let her chisel away. A good activity to be done in the shade on a hot summer day.

Styrofoam Sculptures

The next time you buy something that is packed in styrofoam, save the styrofoam pieces and cut them into interesting shapes. Your child can make an unusual sculpture by sticking toothpicks, popsicle sticks, wire, hairpins, pencils and paper clips into the styrofoam pieces.

Wood Sculptures

Collect an assortment of wood scraps that are different sizes and shapes from your local lumberyard. Your child can glue these pieces together to form an interesting sculpture. He might want to add on cardboard tubes, empty spools, popsicle sticks or pieces of corrugated cardboard.

modeling, mobiles and other things

Play Dough Recipe

Mix together 800 ml (3¼ cups) flour and 240 ml (1 cup) salt. Add 360 ml (1½ cups) water, several drops of food coloring and 15 ml (1 tbsp.) salad oil.

Cornstarch Recipe for Modeling Dough

Mix together 240 ml (1 cup) cornstarch and 360 ml (1½ cups) baking soda. Add 240 ml cold water and several drops of food coloring.

Twig Mobile

Attach a piece of string to an unusually shaped twig. Suspend it from the ceiling or a doorway entrance. From this twig your child can hang any number of different objects . . . like pictures cut from magazines and glued to different shapes of cardboard, play dough objects that have been baked and painted, or different letters, numbers and shapes that have been cut from colored paper and attached to strings.

Bake It and Save It

Either one of the above recipes can be baked after your child has created something she wants to keep forever. Bake the play dough recipe for about 45 minutes at 150° C. (300° F.). Bake the cornstarch recipe for 1½ hours at 120° C. (250° F.). The objects can then be painted with easel paint. Why not hang some of your child's creations on the Christmas tree as ornaments?

Straw Mobile

Let your child cut out interesting shapes from paper. Then with a needle and thread he can alternate stringing different lengths of paper straws and his cut out shapes. Tie a knot after the last shape. These chains can be attached to a hanger. Suspend the hanger from a doorway entrance.

Flying Disc

Cut circles of varying sizes out of stiff paper or cardboard; then cut a narrow pie slice out of the circle. Your child will enjoy tossing them through the air (preferably outside).

44

Fingerprint Stationery

Let your child experiment with using an old stamp pad to make interesting finger prints and thumb prints. Add a few wings, feet or a face and you've got fingerprint creatures. You might want to put these prints on the upper left-hand corner of blank white paper and use the paper as stationery. These fingerprint creatures could also be made on the back flap of the envelopes for the stationery.

Sewing Cards

Punch holes in cardboard pieces which have been cut in various shapes and sizes. Your child can practice lacing in and out the holes with a long colorful shoelace or a piece of yarn (stiffen the ends of the yarn by wrapping tape around them). When he has mastered the ins and outs of this activity, you might want to number the holes so he can follow a particular pattern.

Jigsaw Puzzle

Let your child pick out an interesting picture from an old magazine. Glue this picture onto a piece of cardboard which has been cut the same size. Shellac and cut into a number of interesting pieces to form a puzzle. Your child might also want to make a puzzle out of one of his favorite drawings.

Twirlies

Dip a piece of yarn into a dish of liquid starch. Arrange the yarn in an interesting shape or pattern on a piece of waxed paper. Put another piece of waxed paper on top and flatten between some books. The yarn should be dry and stiff in about 24 hours. Attach a string and suspend in a doorway entrance.

Squeeze Art

Mix together equal parts of flour, salt and water. Add a small amount of liquid tempera paint or food coloring to the mixture and pour it into plastic squeeze bottles, like those used for catsup. Squeeze onto pieces of cardboard or heavy paper. When the designs are dry, the salt gives them a glistening quality. Swirl the colors together for a dazzling effect.

Cork Giraffe

Use a large cork for the body of the giraffe. Legs, neck and tail are made by poking a hairpin through raisins. Add a small cork for the head and brightly colored paper for the eyes, ears and mouth. Now think of other crazy creatures to make.

Goop

Mix together 120 ml (½ cup) cornstarch and 60 ml (¼ cup) water on a cookie sheet that has a small edge around it. Add a drop or two of food coloring. The mixture should be somewhat thick and just barely smooth. Now it is ready to squeeze, drip, swish and play in . . . a very strange texture, indeed. Try it yourself . . . you'll enjoy this gooey delight too!

Silly Putty

Mix together 240 ml 1 (cup) Elmer's glue and 120 ml (½ cup) Sta-Flo liquid starch. This mixture will need to dry slightly before it is pliable. Store it in an airtight container. Silly putty is wonderfully bouncy and will also "lift" comics off a page when it is pressed over them.

Beads

Color elbow or shell macaroni by dipping it into a dish of water and food coloring then drying it on a piece of waxed paper. Your child will enjoy stringing these noodles to make an assortment of necklaces, love beads or bracelets to wear. Necklaces, beads and bracelets can also be made out of empty thread spools, play dough balls or cut-up drinking straws.

Bean Mosaic

Provide your child with an assortment of different dried beans like kidney, pinto or lima. When glued to a piece of cardboard, they make an interesting mosaic.

Scented Ball

Poke cloves into an apple or orange until it is completely covered. Let it stand near a radiator or in the sunlight for three or four days. Tie a ribbon into a bow and attach to the top of the scented ball. This will make a nice gift for a relative or friend to hang in their closet.

Rice Designs

Your child will enjoy dripping glue onto a colored piece of paper into an interesting design. She can then sprinkle rice over the entire paper. Let dry and shake off the excess. Salt, sand or sawdust may also be used.

Popcorn Pictures

Let your child help you make up a batch of popcorn. He can then glue the popcorn (and some unpopped kernels) on a piece of heavy paper or cardboard to make an unusual kind of picture.

Lather-up Fingerpaint

For a quick and easy fingerpaint, squirt out shaving cream onto a cookie sheet. Add a drop or two of food coloring and let your child enjoy the pure sensory pleasure of squishing, squeezing and sliding his fingers and hands through the foam. You can also put this mixture on glossy paper and let him create a picture out of his swirls. This may take a day to dry before you can hang it up for display.

Eggshell Vases

Save those eggshells from your morning breakfast. Dip into food coloring and let dry. Crunch into tiny pieces. Spread glue over the outside of a dark bottle. Sprinkle the crushed eggshells on top of the glue. This makes a beautiful vase to give as a gift.

Pizza Pictures

Cut out a large round circle and let your child color or paint the circle red (this is the sauce). Then provide a small selection of herbs like oregano, basil leaves, thyme, bay leaves, cloves, parsley (or whatever else looks tempting from your spice and herb shelf). Glue these on the pizza pie.

Sand Jars

Next time you visit the beach, take along an empty milk carton or similar container to bring home some fine sand. Divide the sand into separate bowls and sprinkle a small amount of dry tempera into each so that you have a whole kaleidoscope of colors. Then let your child carefully spoon a small amount of each color into a clean baby food jar until the jar is completely full. Cap securely. The rainbow effect will be sure to dazzle both you and your child.

puppets

Egg Head Puppet

Poke a small hole into one end of an uncooked egg. Drain out the contents. Enlarge the hole to fit on your child's finger. Add facial features with colored felt-tipped markers. Glue on pieces of yarn for hair.

Fly Swatter Puppet

Glue wire, foil, cotton or paper features to the flat side of a fly swatter. Manipulate by holding the handle.

Snake

Use an old colorful knee sock. Tuck in the tip of the toe for the snake's mouth and add a piece of red felt for his tongue. Glue or sew on buttons for his eyes.

Felt Puppet

Cut out two identical pieces of felt in the shape indicated. Make sure they are big enough for your child's hand to fit inside. Sew the sides together and glue on features cut from felt scraps.

Flying Ghost

Tie a square piece of sheet or an old handkerchief over a ball of cotton. Features can be added with a black felt-tipped marker. Add a stick inside to make the ghost move or fly him through the air by attaching a piece of string.

Cereal Box Cat

Use a small cereal box. Cut in half on three sides. Fold back leaving two openings to slip thumb and fingers into. Uncut side becomes the mouth. Paint and glue on ears, eyes, nose, tongue and whiskers.

Spoon Puppet

Cut a strip of material that is about 8 cm x 16 cm (3" x 6"). Gather it around the neck of a serving spoon. Secure with a wire or string. Make a face on the back side of the spoon with pieces of construction paper and glue on pieces of yarn for hair.

Paper Plate Bunny

Staple or sew together two paper plates around the edges leaving an opening at the bottom that is large enough for your child's hand to fit into. Cut long ears out of heavy white paper and attach with a stapler. Add features with a black felt-tipped marker or construction paper.

Stuffed Bag Puppet

Let your child make a face on the flat side of a paper bag using crayons or felt-tipped markers. She can then stuff the bag with newspaper and glue yarn pieces on top for hair. Insert a pole or stick at the bottom and tie around the bag with a heavy string.

Caterpillar

Cut a cardboard egg carton lengthwise and turn upside down. Pipe cleaners or a piece of wire may be poked through the front to serve as antennas. Features may be added with crayons, paint or felt-tipped markers.

Paper Bag Puppet

Use the flap of a small bag as the mouth for this puppet. Cut out two small triangles. Glue one triangle under the flap. Glue the other triangle on the flap. Both should be pointing down. Bend the top triangle up to form the puppet's mouth. Add construction paper, crayon or yarn features. Manipulate the puppet by placing hand inside the bag and moving flap.

Stick Puppets

Select characters from a magazine. Let your child cut them out and paste to a tongue depressor or popsicle stick.

Potato Head Puppet

Almost anything can be used to make the face on this puppet . . . tiny marshmallows, cloves, paperclips, tacks or curled wire. His cap is made from the toe of a sock which has been turned up. Stick in a pencil at the bottom of the potato and he's all finished. Carrots, apples and turnips also make interesting puppets. Unfortunately, these puppets have a short life span.

Mitten Man

Tuck thumb of mitten inside. Add features of yarn and buttons. Manipulate this puppet by putting a hand inside the glove.

musical madness

Musical instruments are easy to make and even more fun to play. Invite in a few of your child's playmates and you've got an instant rhythm band . . . . You may decide, however, that this activity is best appreciated from another room!

Shakers

Fill bandage cans, spice cans, baking powder cans or cardboard tubes and boxes with rice, pebbles, beans or marbles and SHAKE, SHAKE, SHAKE.

Guitar

Stretch four or five rubber bands around a shoe box or cigar box. Pluck.

Chimes

Fill glasses with different levels of water and tap lightly on rim.

Humming Comb

Cover a comb with waxed paper and hum on the teeth of the comb.

Sand Blocks

Cut two pieces of 2.5 cm (1") thick wood about 5 cm x 10 cm (2" x 4"). Cut two smaller pieces about 2.5 cm x 5 cm (1" x 2"). Nail or screw the smaller piece onto the larger piece. Cut strips of sandpaper that are 7.5 cm x 13 cm (3" x 5"). Glue them onto the bottoms of the larger blocks. Scrape together.

Rhythm Sticks

Cut two pieces of 12 mm (½") hardwood dowel about 23 cm (9") long. Hit together.

Horn

Blow gently into the top of an empty soda bottle.

Tambourine

Staple together two pie tins. Sew on bells or bottle caps or fill with small stones. Shake.

Cymbals

Strike two pan lids against one another.

Ringer

Suspend a fork, spoon or horseshoe from a string and tap lightly with a fork.

Coconut Clankers

Saw a coconut in half and clean out the inside. When the two halves are tapped together, they make an interesting galloping sound.

Rattles

Drill a hole through one end of a tongue depressor or popsicle stick. With a piece of wire, attach two or three bells to the stick. Shake. Instead of bells, you can also use bottle caps that have had a hole punched through the center with an ice pick. Attach to the stick with a wire.

Gong

Suspend a pot lid by a string and hit with a large metal spoon.

Drums

Stretch a piece of canvas, rubber tubing from an old tire or a thick piece of balloon across the top of a small barrel, a large coffee can or an oatmeal box. Secure by lacing, nailing or gluing to the side of the drum.

creating through art and music★★★★★

For the adult:

Bently, W.G. *Learning To Move and Moving to Learn* (New York: Citation Press, 1970). Excellent resource and very moving!

Birkenshow, Lois. *Music For Fun, Music For Learning* (Toronto, Ontario,: Holt, Rinehart and Winston, 1975). Good collection of movement activities, ideas for rhythms and games, and songs for children to sing.

Cherry, Clare. *Creative Art For the Developing Child: a Teacher's Handbook For Early Childhood Education* (Belmont, Calif.: Fearon Publishing Co., 1972). Excellent survey of methods and materials.

Cobb, Vickie. *Arts and Crafts You Can Eat* (New York: Lippincott, 1972). Geared for older children but can be adapted for preschoolers as well.

Katz, Pat. *Sandcastles and Snowflakes* (Walnut Creek, Calif.: MAD Publishing Co., 1980). Easy to use format and especially good for toddlers.

Kellogg, Rhoda. *Analyzing Children's Art* (Plato Alto, Calif.: Mayfield Publishing Co., 1970). Traces the artistic development of children from two to eight, defining and classifying the forms common to children's art throughtout the world.

Lowenfeld, V. *Your Child and His Art* (New York: Macmillan, 1965). A must to include on your reading list.

Proudzinski, John. *It's a Small, Small World But Larger Than You Think* (Washington, D.C.: Day Care & Child Development Council of America). A collection of songs, chants and movement activities to do with young children. Specifically designed for the non-musician.

Rogers, Fred. *Mister Rogers' Songbook* (New York: Random House, 1970). Collection of favorite songs from the popular children's television show.

Stecher, Miriam B. *Music and Movement Improvisation,* Threshold Early Learning Library, vol. 4 (New York: Macmillan, 1972). Candid snapshots, ancedotes and concrete suggestions.

Williamson, Ethie. *Baker's Clay* (New York: Van Nostrand, Reinhold Co., 1976). Cutouts, sculptures and projects with flour, salt and water.

Young, Milton A. *Buttons Are To Push* (New York: Pitman, 1970). Developing your child's creativity.

For the child:

Carr, Rachel. *Be a Frog, a Bird Or a Tree* (Doubleday, 1973). Photographs illustrate simple yoga exercises with drawings of the animals that children are imitating.

Diskin, Eve. *Yoga For Children* (Arco Publishing Co. 1976). Exercises are sequenced into levels of difficulty for children of all ages.

Doray, Maya. *See What I Can Do! a Book Of Creative Movement* (Prentice-Hall, 1974). Simple, well-illustrated movements for young children to imitate.

Sources of records for children: (Write for catalogs)

Children's Music Center	Folkways Records
2558 East Pico Boulevard	165 West 46th Street
Los Angeles, California 90019	New York, New York 10036
Kimbo Educational Records	Young People's Records, Inc.
P.O. Box 246	100 Fifth Avenue
Deal, New Jersey 07723	New York, New York 10011

what's cooking

There are many things children can do in the kitchen that will not only instill valuable learning skills but will also be of help to you. They can help you scrub potatoes, set the table, sift flour, grate or chop vegetables, pour milk from a small pitcher, season food, peel hard-boiled eggs and assist in making simple dishes. In fact, one of the fastest ways to get an uncooperative eater to eat more is to let the child assist you in preparing the meal.

The recipes on the following pages are included because they are tasty, nutritious and easy to make. It is up to you, however, to decide just how much assistance your child will need. Too much responsibility can be overwhelming, too little can make an activity boring. While you are in the kitchen together, talk about the taste, texture and color of different foods. This will make the experience far more educational and meaningful for the child. Doing cooking experiences together provides the perfect opportunity for you to teach the essentials of kitchen safety as well. Be sure to caution children about the hazards of hot stoves, small appliances and sharp utensils. You'll both be thankful!

Breakfast On a String

The next time you're going to have Cheerios for breakfast, pour an extra bowl for your child and round up a long piece of yarn or string. Wrap a small piece of tape around one end of the string to make lacing the Cheerios easier. Tie one Cheerio to the other end of the string to keep the rest of them from slipping off. When your child has finished stringing all the Cheerios, you can tie the two ends together. A perfect necklace to munch on during the day!

Pancake Alphabet

Use your favorite pancake recipe or try these light and fluffy cottage cheese pancakes.

    4 eggs, separated
    1 cup (240 ml) cottage cheese
    ½ cup (120 ml) sifted flour
    2 T. (30 ml) salad oil
        salt

Using an electric or hand mixer, combine the cottage cheese and egg yolks until smooth. Add the flour, salt and salad oil. In a separate bowl, whip the egg whites until stiff. Fold the egg whites into the cottage cheese mixture. Pour into a squeeze bottle or drip unto a hot, greased griddle. Best to begin with simple letters like T, H, U, O. Cook until bubbles appear, then turn and brown on the other side. Once you've perfected your griddle-writing talents, try creating simple animals with the batter like a turtle or fish. Children will gobble these up.

Applesauce

    6 tart apples
    ½ cup (120 ml) sugar
    1½ cups (360 ml) water
    2 t. (10 ml) cinnamon

Help your child peel, core and chop the apples. Cover with water in a saucepan and add the cinnamon and sugar. Simmer until tender. Serve warm on pancakes or try the following recipe for an interesting variation.

Apple White

Whip two egg whites until stiff. Add 1½ cups (360 ml) applesauce and the juice of one small lemon. Whip a few minutes longer. Serve on toast for an interesting morning treat.

Tutti-Fruiti Energy Drink

    1 small can orange juice concentrate
    1 banana
    1 t. (5 ml) vanilla
    1 T. (15 ml) honey
    1 cup unflavored or flavored yogurt
    1 egg
    ½ cup (120 ml) water
    fresh or frozen strawberries or peaches
    crushed ice

Combine all ingredients in a blender and whip until smooth. This will make enough for the whole family to enjoy.

Children are more cooperative eaters when they have a chance to select and make choices about what they eat. Here are some snacks and lunchtime favorites that they'll love to assemble and eat . . . so make sure you have plenty around for seconds.

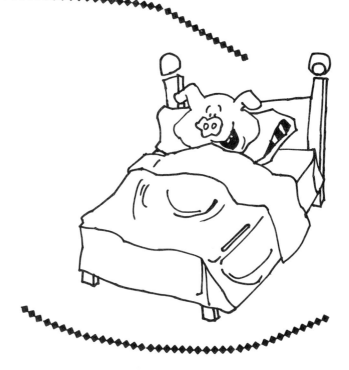

Pigs In a Blanket

240 ml (1 cup) Bisquick
60 ml (¼ cup) water
6 hot dogs

Mix Bisquick and water to form dough. Roll out into circle. Cut into six pie-shaped slices. Place hot dogs at wide end of each slice and roll up. Place on an ungreased cookie sheet and bake for 15 minutes at 230°C. (450°F.).

Mini Pizzi

Spread 1 T. (15 ml) tomato sauce on ½ English muffin and let your child top with her favorites. Some possibilities: chopped mushrooms, onions, black olives, green peppers, grated mozzarella or Monterey Jack cheese. Slip under the broiler for a few minutes until cheese is melted.

Fruit Kabob

Let your child select three or four different fruits that are firm and not too juicy . . . apples, pears, peaches, strawberries and oranges work well. Together peel and cut the fruit into chunks. Your child will delight in arranging a colorful fruit pattern on a wooden skewer. (These are available in most grocery stores in the gourmet section.) After the fruit is on the skewer, you might want to snip off the point. Kabobs make fun hors d'oeuvres for grown-up parties, too . . . and your child will be sure to want to assist in the preparation.

Make a Facewich

With a round cookie cutter, let your child cut out a circle from a slice of whole-wheat bread. Then spread on some peanut butter or soft cream cheese. This is where the fun begins . . . Set up a small mirror on the table for your child to look into and talk about her eyes, nose, mouth and hair. Then using a little ingenuity, together assemble the makings . . . raisins, sliced olives, almonds, chopped dates, sunflower seeds, alfalfa sprouts, carrot curls and whatever else you can dream up to create a face.

Easy and Economic . . . Eggs

Here are three versatile recipes that kids really go for:

Egg Salad Roll-Ups

3 hard-boiled eggs
1 stalk celery, chopped
3 T. (45 ml) sweet pickle relish
3 T. (45 ml) mayonnaise
salt and pepper
flour tortillas

Let your child peel and mash the eggs. Add the celery, relish, mayonnaise, salt and pepper. Spread on a flour tortilla and roll up. Somewhat messy to eat, but children don't seem to mind!

Egg and Veggie Scramble

For each person, beat together:

1 egg
½ t. (2 ml) soy sauce
pinch of salt

Add any three:

1 T. (15 ml) chopped celery
1 T. chopped green onion
1 T. chopped mushrooms
1 T. chopped carrot
1 T. grated cabbage
1 T. bean sprouts

Fry on a greased griddle until firm. This is a wonderful recipe for children because each combination of veggies looks and tastes different, so there will be *some* combination that will please *every* child.

Magic Eggs

3 slices whole-wheat bread
3 eggs
margarine
salt and pepper

Help your child cut a hole in the middle of each slice of bread with a 2″ (5 cm) biscuit or cookie cutter. On a hot griddle, fry each slice in a small amount of margarine until golden brown. Turn. Carefully break an egg into the center of the hole. Salt and pepper to taste. Fry for about 3 minutes until egg is firm. Slip onto a plate.

Cheese Pretzels

1 T. (15 ml) active dry yeast
1½ cups (360 ml) warm water
1 t. (5 ml) salt
1 t. (5 ml) sugar
3 cups (720 ml) whole-wheat flour
1½ cups (360 ml) grated sharp cheddar cheese
1 egg, beaten

Dissolve the yeast in the warm water in a large bowl. Stir in salt and sugar. Add the flour and the cheese. Mix well. Knead the dough on a floured surface until smooth. Cut off pieces and help your child roll thin cords to shape into pretzels, breadsticks, circles, numbers or his initials. Place on an ungreased cookie sheet. Brush with beaten egg and sprinkle with sesame seeds, poppy seeds or large-grain (kosher) salt. Bake 10-15 minutes at 375° F. (190° C.). Makes about 32 "average" sized pretzels.

Thumb Pies

1 cup (240 ml) whole-wheat flour
½ t. (2 ml) salt
¼ cup (60 ml) margarine
1 T. (15 ml) honey
2 T. [3] ml) water

Mix all ingredients well. Let your child form into little balls. (If the mixture is too flaky, add a little more water). Make a thumb print in each ball. Place on a greased cookie sheet and bake at 350° F. (175° C.) for 8-10 minutes. Fill the holes with fruit jelly, preserves or peanut butter.

Finger Jello

4 envelopes unflavored gelatin
2 cups (480 ml) orange juice
¾ cup (180 ml) boiling water

Sprinkle the gelatin over ½ cup of the orange juice in a bowl. Add the boiling water and stir until the gelatin dissolves. Add the remaining juice and pour into a 9″ (23 cm) pan. Chill until firm. Slice with a warm knife into cubes. Makes 5-6 dozen squares. Kids love the texture and the taste!

Fortune Cookies

3 egg whites
¾ cup (180 ml) sugar
dash of salt
½ t. (2 ml) vanilla
½ cup (120 ml) butter
2 T. (30 ml) strong tea
1 cup (240 ml) flour

Collaborate with your child to think up some funny and amusing fortunes. Write or type these on small strips of paper. Beat together the sugar and egg whites until fluffy. Melt the butter and cool until just warm. Add the flour, salt, tea, vanilla and the egg mixture. Mix until the batter is smooth. Chill for 30 minutes. Spoon onto a heavily greased cookie sheet in the form of small circles about 3½″ (8 cm) wide. Bake at 375° F. (190° C.) for about 5 minutes. Lay a message on each circle, fold into thirds, then bend gently in the center. As cookies must be shaped when they're warm, it's best to bake only 2 or 3 at a time. If a cookie gets too hard to bend, rewarm it for a minute or so.

Toasted Hearts Delight

With a heart-shaped cookie cutter, let your child cut out a heart shape from a slice of whole-wheat toast. Mix together softened cream cheese and strawberry or cherry preserves. Spread the mixture on the heart . . . and eat to your heart's delight.

Protein-Packed Peanut Butter

2 cups (480 ml) shelled peanuts
¼ cup (60 ml) vegetable oil
1 t. (5 ml) slat

Put all ingredients into a blender and whip until smooth. Store in refrigerator.

Peanut Crunchies

1 cup (240 ml) peanut butter
¼ cup (60 ml) dry milk
1¼ cups (300 ml) puffed wheat or puffed rice cereal
¼ cup (60 ml) chopped nuts

Stir together peanut butter, honey and dry milk. Add the puffed cereal and chopped nuts. Mix well. Press into a square pan and refrigerate until firm. Cut into squares. This mixture can also be frozen for an even crunchier taste.

Peanut-Raisin Bread

2 cups (480 ml) enriched flour
1 T. (15 ml) baking powder
1 t. (5 ml) slat
¼ cup (60 ml) brown sugar
1½ cups (360 ml) milk
¾ cup (180 ml) peanut butter
½ cup (120 ml) raisins.

Mix together flour, baking powder, salt, sugar and raisins in a bowl. Set aside. Blend together milk and peanut butter. Add the peanut butter mixture to the dry ingredients and mix well. Pour into a greased loaf pan and bake at 350°F. (175°C.) for 50 minutes.

Popcorn . . . and Popular Variations

Use an electric popper to pop up some popcorn. Let your child examine the kernels of corn before popping. Then let him try to float a kernel before and after it has been popped. Make some homemade butter to put on the popcorn. Add a little salt.

For a tasty treat, add any of your child's favorites and divide into small baggies for snack-attacks. Some possibilities: raisins, nuts, sunflower seeds, cheese bits, broken pretzels, dates, dried fruit, rice or corn chex, miniature shredded wheat cereal.

Butter

Help your child pour some heavy cream into a clean baby food jar. Screw on the lid very tight and then shake, shake, shake. Watch the lumps form. Pour off the liquid (buttermilk) and add a pinch of salt. Refrigerate.

Carob-Oatmeal Drops

2 T. (30 ml) carob powder
¼ cup (60 ml) milk
¼ cup (60 ml) margarine
1½ cups (360 ml) oatmeal
½ cup (120 ml) peanut butter
½ cup brown sugar

Mix the carob powder and milk until smooth. Stir in the margarine and sugar. Heat until boiling for 1 minute. Remove from heat. Add the oatmeal and peanut butter. Mix well and drop by teaspoonfuls onto waxed paper. Chill until firm. Makes 2 dozen.

Fruit Leather

Good with plums, peaches and apricots that are extra ripe. Cover the ripe fruit with water and simmer until soft. Drain off liquid and press through a collander. Sweeten to taste and pour onto a greased cookie sheet. Bake at 250° F. (120° C.) until dry. Cut into strips and roll in plastic wrap to store.

Alphabet Soup

2 cans stewed tomatoes
1 cup (240 ml) tomato juice
1 cup (240 ml) water
1 carrot, chopped
1 stalk celery, chopped
1 small onion, chopped
1 small can of corn or peas
1 bay leaf
¼ cup (60 ml) alphabet soup noodles
salt, pepper, parsley and sweet basil to taste

Assist your child in chopping the vegetables and putting all the ingredients into a large pot. Simmer for 1 hour.

Apple, Celery and Carrot Salad

4 apples, chopped
2 stalks celery, chopped
1 grated carrot
2 T. (30 ml) plain yogurt
2 T. (30 ml) mayonnaise
¼ cup (60 ml) raisins
salt and pepper

Help your child put all the ingredients into a large bowl and mix well.

Banana Pops

2 bananas

Carob coating:

   ¼ cup (60 ml) carob powder

   1 t. (5 ml) vanilla

   1 T. (15 ml) honey

   2 T. (30 ml) milk or cream

toppings:

   toasted wheat germ

   chopped walnuts or peanuts

   flaked coconut

   granola

Let your child peel the bananas. Then cut each in half crosswise and insert a popsicle stick in the cut end. Combine the ingredients for the carob coating and mix until smooth. Your child can then dip each banana pop into the coating and roll in one (or all) of the crunch toppings. Freeze.

Yumsicles

1 cup unflavored yogurt

1 small can orange or grape juice concentrate

1 T. (15 ml) honey

½ t. (2 ml) vanilla

Mix ingredients together and spoon into molds or small paper cups. Freeze partially, then insert a wooden stick into each. Freeze until firm. When ready to eat, peel off the paper cup. These yumsicles are not only nutritious, but they're easy and neat for children to handle.

Parent: Please remind your child that running while eating a yumsicle or banana pop can be *very* dangerous. You may even want to use plastic straws cut in half as holders for these treats rather than wooden sticks.

Nutty Treat

800 ml (3¼ cups) oatmeal

240 ml (1 cup) unsweetened coconut

240 ml (1 cup) toasted wheat germ

240 ml (1 cup) favorite chopped nuts

  (like almonds or walnuts)

240 ml (1 cup) honey

60 ml (½ cup) melted butter

Preheat oven to 150° C. (300° F.). Combine oatmeal, coconut, wheat germ and nuts in a bowl. Heat honey and butter. Pour over dry ingredients. Spread on a cookie sheet. Toast in oven for 15-20 minutes.

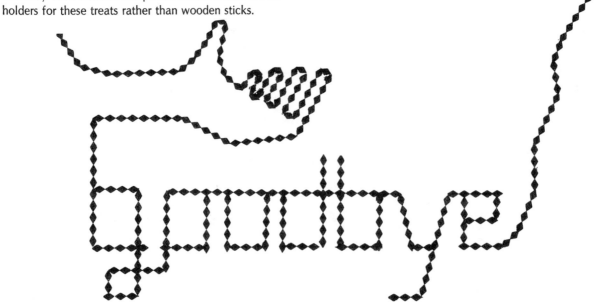

what's cooking••

For the adult:

Burns, Marilyn. *Good For Me!* (Boston: Little, Brown & Co., 1978).

Endres, Jeannette. *Food, Nutrition, and the Young Child* (St. Louis, Mo.: Mosby, 1980). Focuses upon nutrition as an integral part of early childhood programs and examines curriculum approaches for effective nutrition education.

Lappe, Frances Moore. *Diet For a Small Planet* (New York: Ballantine, 1975). Bringing protein theory down to earth.

Pipes, Peggy L. *Nutrition In Infancy and Childhood.* (St. Louis: Mosby, 1977). Theoretical and practical information about nutritional sources, food intake and feeding behavior of young children.

Additional resources for nutrition education:

Consumer Information Center
Pueblo, Colorado 81009

Food and Nutrition Information and
   Education Materials Center
Nutrition Agricultural Library
Room 304
Beltsville, Maryland 20705

National Dairy Council
111 N. Canal Street
Chicago, Illinois 60605

Society for Nutrition Education
2140 Shattuck Avenue
Suite 1110
Berkeley, California 94704

Cookbooks with recipes that appeal to young children:

Cavin, Ruth. *1 Pinch Of Sunshine, 1/2 Cup Of Rain: Natural Food Recipes For Young People* (New York: Atheneum, 1973).

Cooper, Jane. *Love At First Bite* (New York: Alfred Knopf, 1977). Snacks and mealtime treats the quick and easy way.

Croft, Karen. *The Good For Me Cookbook* (San Francisco: R & E Research Associates, 1971). Emphasis on healthful, nutritious recipes that cover a wide range of foods from different ethnic groups.

Goodwin, Mary. *Creative Food Experiences For Children* (Washington, D.C.: Center for Science in the Public Interest, 1974). An indispensable resource guide for nutrition education for young children. Well organized, thorough and very informative.

Lansky, Vicki. *Taming the C.A.N.D.Y. Monster* (Deephaven, Minn.: Meadowbrook Press, 1976). Helping kids kick the junk-food habit.

Lewin, Esther. *Growing Food — Growing Up — a Child's Natural Food Book* (Pasadena, Calif.: Ward Ritchie Press, 1977). Well-illustrated step-by-step approach to nutrition education.

Parent's Nursery School. *Kids Are Natural Cooks* (Boston: Houghton Mifflin, 1974). Nutritious recipes with a sense of humor. Lively illustrations.

Petrich, Patricia. *The Kid's Cookbook* (Concord, Calif.: Nitty Gritty Books, 1973). An interesting collection of recipes that have been child-tested!

Smith, Lendon. *Feed Your Kids Right* (New York: Delta Books, 1979). A program for your child's total health.

what's cooking••••••••••••••••••••••••••••••••••••••

Storybooks that promote an interest in cooking and nutrition:

Brown, Marcia. *Stone Soup* (Charles Scribner & Sons).

Hoban, Russell. *Bread and Jam For Frances* (Harper & Row, 1970).

Krauss, Ruth. *La Semilla De Zanahoria* (Scholastic, 1975). The Spanish edition of THE CARROT SEED.

Krantz, Hazel. *100 Pounds Of Popcorn* (Vanguard, 1961).

McCloskey, Robert. *Blueberries For Sal* (Viking, 1948).

Sendak, Maurice. *Chicken Soup With Rice* (Harper & Row, 1962).

Sendak, Maurice. *In the Night Kitchen* (Harper & Row, 1970).

Seuss, Dr. *Green Eggs and Ham* (Random House, 1960).

Seuss, Dr. *Scrambled Eggs Super* (Random House, 1953).

Wondriska, William. *The Tomato Patch* (Holt, Rinehart & Winston, 1969).

teacher's supplement

Dear Teacher,

A quick look at the contents of LIVING & LEARNING WITH CHILDREN will show you that it is a valuable curriculum aid for any early childhood education program. Remember, however, that this book was not designed to be followed activity by activity. Rather, it should be used by the creative teacher as a resource tool from which to draw, expand and generate new ideas tailored to the specific needs of students.

In using a resource book such as this, keep in mind that a child's learning is relative to the degree of involvement in the learning task. Involvement comes when activities are relevant and meaningful to each child's changing interests and developmental needs. The most important ingredient in this learning process is the child's self-image as a learner. If children have repeated experiences in seeking, doing and achieving, then they will gradually derive a sense of self-esteem and a feeling of competence that breeds success and motivation for future learning. The skillful teacher, then, will develop a curriculum that provides many learning experiences that nurture the child's emerging self-concept and foster self reliance.

One way this is accomplished is to key the curriculum to the seemingly insignificant day-to-day occurrences experienced by the child. For example, if a child in your class came to school with a bag full of old bones, a bird's egg, or a dead worm, would you be flexible enough to jetison planned activities in favor of those that enhanced and amplified the child's new-found interest? What resources and activities would you be able to draw upon if the electricity went out in your classroom, if a spider walked across your path during storytime, or if a child lost her first tooth during snack? The ways in which you are able to build upon such events and develop them into rewarding educational experiences will determine whether your students become active agents in their education or passive recipients of your teacher-directed tasks.

LIVING & LEARNING WITH CHILDREN provides a framework for approaching each new incident, event, or commonplace object that makes its way into your educational domain. Ask yourself in what ways the experience can be related to the different chapters in this book on sensory awareness, reading readiness, math, science, art, music and cooking. Be inventive. Be spontaneous. And most of all, be flexible enough to drop an activity if it's going poorly. The teacher who generates a curriculum from the children's sparks of enthusiasm inevitably works harder and sleeps less, not knowing exactly what to expect the following day. But the fire grows because a powerful message is conveyed to children that they are important individuals whose thoughts, feelings and emotions are significant and worthwhile. Such feelings enhance their self-image and cultivate curiousity and awareness of the world. Should the teacher of young children aim for anything less?

Another way that the skillful teacher fosters the child's self-concept is to weave a number of self-awareness activities into the curriculum. Because such activities appeal to the young child's egocentric nature, they help foster a better sense of self in relation to the external world. Described below are a number of activities that focus on self-awareness. Try to incorporate as many as possible into your curriculum. Because they center on the child's most personal world they will be both highly rewarding for the child as well as facilitate a healthy self-concept. Many are keyed to the pages of LIVING & LEARNING WITH CHILDREN.

ACTIVITIES THAT BUILD SELF-AWARENESS

1. The child's name. What is more personal than a child's name? Use it often! The following activities let the child know his or her name is important. Capitalize on this enthusiasm by instilling important cognitive skills of letter recognition and auditory discrimination as well.

First, Middle, last name cards: (page 15)

Name rub: Drip white glue on a stiff card or small piece of cardboard to form the letters of each child's name. Let the glue dry for several days. Children will be able to magically make their name appear by laying a piece of paper over the name card and rubbing lightly with the flat side of a crayon.

Loony letters: (page 11)

Letter collage: (page 11)

Coil a letter: (page 10)

Rice name: Let the children spread glue on a piece of stiff paper or cardboard to form the letters of their name. Sprinkle rice on top (sand and cornmeal also work well) and shake off the excess. Many children will benefit from the opportunity to feel the shape of their name in addition to the visual stimuli.

Sandpaper letters: (page 10)

Name puzzle: In very bold letters write each child's name on a cardboard strip allowing space between each letter for cutting. Make the cuts curved or jagged so that they can only be assembled in the proper sequence. This puzzle can also be made in the shape of a caterpillar, worm or train.

Alpha-bits cereal name collage: (page 10)

Hand talk: Clap out the syllables of each child's name with appropriate emphasis. Soon the children will be able to compare the beat patterns between different names.

Eat a name: Try the recipe for personalized pancakes or cheese pretzels. Your children will enjoy nibbling on their initials, or if they're really hungry, their whole name. If you want to preserve the letters of their name, use the recipe for play dough on page 44 instead. Once these letters are baked they can be painted and decorated and used in a variety of name-game activities.

Cork stamps: Draw the mirror image of an alphabet letter on the bottom of an old cork. Cut away around the letter so that the impression is raised. Press on an inked stamp pad or in a tray of paint and print onto paper. A delightful way to make personalized stationery.

2. The child's concept of body. The way in which children view and understand their bodies has an impact on their over-all self-image. The emphasis in the following activities should always be on the individuality of each child, not on how children compare with one another.

Mirrors, mirrors everywhere: Hang them high, hang them low. Tape expression cards next to mirrors of various shapes. Soon the children will be reading the words and acting out the appropriate expressions. Smile, frown, wink!

Self portrait: Have each child stand before a full-length mirror and examine different aspects of his or her body (eye color, shape of ears, nose, head, etc.). Then each child can color a self portrait keeping those details in mind. This is a good activity to do in September and again in June. Children can then compare the two pictures and note their progress. Attach this poem to each self portrait:

> I looked in the mirror
> And what did I see?
> A very special person . . .
> And that person was ME!

Body talk: Play games that involve using the body instead of words to convey different thoughts. For example: "I'm tired," "Come here," "No."

Preschool physiology 001: Let the children listen to their heart beat with a stethoscope. Stick out tongues at one another and examine each other's taste buds with small magnifying glasses. Demonstrate how knee reflexes work. Have the class lie down on the floor and have each child put one ear on another child's stomach to listen for a growl. Watch the pupil in a child's eye dilate when a flashlight is directed on it in a dark room (teacher controlled, of course). Examine hair, skin or fingernails under a microscope.

Silhouette cut-outs: Cast a child's shadow onto a piece of black construction paper. Trace around and cut out. Glue the silhouette to a larger piece of white paper. Makes a good gift for Valentine's Day.

Body movement exercises: Movement activities that focus on different parts of the body and what each can do (go limp like spaghetti, stiff like a board, etc.) are excellent for instilling an awareness of self. Children can make different shapes or letters with their bodies working either separately or together in small groups. The possibilities for ex-

tending the child's imagination through movement activities are unlimited. Here are just a few:

- Pretend you're a marionette and someone is pulling your strings to make you dance, leap, fall, wave, etc.
- Pretend you're a bouncing ball, a rolling ball, a deflated ball.
- Pretend your arms are two magnets pulling at one another.
- Pretend your head is made out of steel and is very, very heavy.
- Pretend you're a bowl full of jello.
- Pretend you're a rubber band being stretched.

Body puzzle: (page 13)

Weigh and record: (page 24) Do periodically throughout the year. Record results and talk about growth.

Box people: (page 41) Make a whole class.

Photographs: Display photographs of the children engaged in different activities (enlargements are super if you can afford them). The children will be very eager to dictate stories about their friends. Type these dictations and attach to the photographs. The children will be able to read back their dictations in no time at all. Baby photographs are also excellent for prompting discussions about growth and development.

Tape recordings: Children are instantly captivated by the tape recorder. After their initial silliness in hearing themselves, the tape recorder can become a valuable tool, particularly for helping shy children express themselves more fluently.

Shadow play: (page 34)

Tempera footprints and handprints: (page 38)

Plaster of Paris handprints: Mix plaster of Paris according to directions on package. Grease a small pie tin with vaseline. Pour in the plaster of Paris mixture and wait until semi-mushy. Press hand down for a few moments. Let print dry and pop the mold out of the pie tin. Makes a great gift!

Feel it on your toes: (page 4)

Footprint numbers: (page 20)

Foot book: Trace around each child's foot several times. Let the child cut out the feet and attach together at the heel to form the pages of a book. The child can dictate a story about feet on the different

pages. Make a cover and title "My Foot Book." Try also a book about hands or other body parts.

Back tracing: (page 11)

Fingerprints: (page 45) Or make a mixture of baking soda and carbon (available at hardware store). Spread the powder on a glass or dish that a child has handled. Brush off lightly to reveal fingerprints.

Hand print momento: A perfect gift for Mother's Day or Father's Day. Have each child press the palms of their hands in a small tray of paint then make a print on a sheet of construction paper (or a card). Attach the following poem to complete:

> You clean my prints
> From wall and door,
> For I'm not careful
> When I play.
> But here's a print
> I hope you'll keep
> On this special Mother's Day.

Hand cookie: Make up a batch of your favorite cookie dough. Roll out the dough and let your students carve out the outline of their hand on the dough. Bake and munch.

I spy: To make a great (and inexpensive) set of binoculars, take two empty cardboard toilet paper rolls and staple together. Attach a string at one end

so that the binoculars can be carried around the neck. The other ends of the tubes can be covered with colored cellophane paper if you want the world to look rosy, green, blue or yellow.

A nose knows: Make a nose collage by cutting out all the noses that children can find in magazines. Animal noses will give your collage a humorous touch, to be sure, but also help children understand that noses (as well as eyes, ears, etc.) come in very different shapes and sizes. How about a smile collage, too.

Action songs and routines: Songs like "Hokey Pokey," fingerplays or activity records that involve making the body respond to different cues and commands are good for instilling concepts of laterality and directionality. Buzz Glass and Ella Jenkins put out some excellent records in this area.

Stories and books about the body: For example, *Inside You & Me,* Eloise Turner, *Whom Am I?,* June Behrens, *My Book About Me,* Dr. Seuss and many many others.

Me cubes: Find a small square box about 3″ (8 cm) on each side. Tape closed and wrap in plain paper. Now collect six different photographs or small drawings done by a child and glue one onto each side of the cube. You might want to cover the cube with clear contact paper to preserve the pictures. A perfect gift for Valentine's Day.

3. The child's feelings and emotions. Teachers of early childhood education must strive to provide the kind of supportive atmosphere that encourages children to talk openly about their fears, wishes, fantasies and dreams. It is only when children begin to understand their vast array of emotions that they can begin to deal with associated behaviors in mature responsible ways.

Stories: Children are automatically drawn to stories that portray events and situations they can readily identify with. These stories can be used very effectively as a springboard for group discussions about different feelings and emotions. An example of some books that fall into this category are: *Feelings, Inside You and Outloud Too,* Barbara Kay Pollard, *Will I Have a Friend,* Miriam Cohen, *Lost & Found,* Kathryn Hitte, *It's Mine—A Greedy Book,* Crosby Bonsell, *Benjy's Blanket,* Myra B. Brown, *The Quarreling Book,* Charlotte Zolotow, *Ira Sleeps Over,* Bernard Waber.

Group discussions: If group discussions are conducted in a nonjudgmental, nonthreatening manner, children will openly share their thoughts and feelings with others. Some topics for discussion might be the following:

    — More than anything else, I'm afraid of . . .

    — I find it very hard to . . .

    — I wish I could eat one million . . .

    — My scariest dream was about . . .

    — I wish that I could . . .

    — I get very angry when . . .

You're special: There are many ways that we can put the spotlight on individual children during the course of the school year so that each child in a class will feel truly special. How about starting a *Child of the Week* program where one child each week of the school year is highlighted. Some possible activities that might develop would include the following:

    — Having that special child bring in his photo album to share with the class or display his "history" on a bulletin board (pictures of his parents, pets, siblings, favorite toy, places he's visited, etc.).

    — Have his classmates all draw pictures of him along with their dictations about why he is special to them.

    — Let him assist as the teacher's helper during the course of the week, running errands, organizing and cleaning before and after school with the teacher.

    — Perhaps arrange a visit to his house (if his parents are accommodating) to tour his bedroom, play in his yard, and see his special toys.

Birthday celebrations: For the young child, a birthday is the most important day in the year. Yet some children are very perplexed because they don't somehow transform during that magical 24-hour period. Many good discussions can be generated from birthday feelings.

How do you feel? (page 14)

Dream pictures: Have the children color pictures and dictate stories to you about their dreams. These may be very insightful or completely misleading, so don't take them *too* seriously. Also read to the children *A Child's Book of Dreams* by Beatrice Schenk de Regniers.

Things I like and things I don't like: Countless projects for graphs, books and charts can be generated from the child's likes and dislikes. For example, "Foods I like," "My favorite television program," "My favorite wild beast," or "Things I can't live without."

"Dear Me" letters: Let the children write, dictate or scribble a letter to themselves. Address envelopes and mail to their respective homes.

Records: Several recording artists have recently put out albums with songs that are specifically geared to helping the young child build a healthy self-concept. The following are especially noteworthy:

    Hap Palmer, *Getting To Know Myself*
    Marcia Berman and Patty Zeitlin, *Everybody Cries Sometimes*
    Marlo Thomas, *Free To Be . . . You and Me*
    Youngheart Music Group, *We All Live Together*

BOOKS OF GENERAL INTEREST TO PARENTS AND TEACHERS . . .

Here's a diverse dozen you'll definitely want to add to your bookshelf:

Ames, Louise Bates. *Stop School Failure* (New York: Harper & Row, 1972). Stresses the importance of the parent in identifying and correcting potential causes of school failure. Worthwhile reading before a child formally enters school.

Blake, Jim, and Earnst, Barbara. *The Great Perpetual Learning Machine* (Boston: Little, Brown and Company, 1976). A wonderful collection of ideas, games, experiments and activities for home or classroom.

Cohen, Dorothy. *The Learning Child* (New York: Vintage/Random House, 1973). Self-esteem as an antecedent to success in school.

Croft, Doreen, and Hess, Robert. *An Activities Handbook For Teachers Of Young Children,* 2nd ed. (Boston: Houghton Mifflin, 1975). Practical activities drawn from actual classroom use in the areas of science, art, music math, cooking and language.

Eliason, Claudia. *A Practical Guide To Early Childhood Curriculum* (St. Louis: Mosby, 1977). Well-organized presentation of child-centered activities.

Flemming, Bonnie, Hamilton, Darlene, and Hicks, JoAnne. *Resources For Creative Teaching In Early Childhood Education* (New York: Harcourt Brace and Jovanovich, 1977). Superb resource handbook for developing curriculum themes and units of study.

Fraiberg, Selma. *The Magic Years* (New York: Charles Scribner, 1959). To be read and reread and reread again!

Jones, Sandy. *Learning For Little Kids* (Boston: Houghton Mifflin, 1979). Excellent resource book for parents as well as teachers.

Lorton, Mary Baratta. *Workjobs* (Menlo Park, Calif.: Addison-Wesley, 1973). Well photographed guide to making learning games from simple materials for home or classroom.

Scharlatt, Elisabeth. Ed., *Kids Day In and Day Out* (New York: Simon & Schuster, 1979). Very comprehensive resource manual for parents and teachers.

Sprung, Barbara. *Non-Sexist Education For Young Children: A Practical Guide* (New York: Citation Press, 1975). Includes annotated bibliographies of nonsexist picture books and curriculum materials for the preschool years.

Seefeldt, Carol. A Curriculum For Child Care Centers (Columbus, Ohio: Charles Merrill, 1973). An indispensable guide for the new teacher. Well-written, thorough, and easy to use.

Suggested Reading
Available at bookstores everywhere

If unavailable through your bookseller, you may order
directly from the publisher, Acropolis Books, Ltd.

Parent Tricks-Of-The-Trade

For The First Ten Years
1,001 Time and Money-Saving Solutions
All Child-tested

by Kathleen Touw
illustrated by Loel Barr

Busy, harried parents — experienced and inexperienced — will find here hundreds of time and money-saving solutions to common problems of raising children.

PARENT TRICKS-OF-THE-TRADE begins when you find yourself pregnant with hints for making yourself comfortable, preparing a room for the baby, even what to give and hope-for in baby gifts.

Then you'll find scores of tips when you are at home with your newborn: from feeding and diapers to first teeth.

Learn how to find room for all those toys, how to decorate the playroom and the bedroom as your child grows up, how to bathe her and shampoo her and keep her nails cut.

Discover soothing solutions to fears, sibling rivalry, discipline problems, and loss.

Find out how to cope and care for bumps, bangs, moans and groans, how to make doctor's and dentist's visits less frightening, how to keep your child's environment safe and what to do in case of emergencies.

Discover games, activities, crafts, gifts, books to read to them, plus holiday and birthday party activities, how to travel on short trips to town or long trips in the car.

And, last but not least, you'll find myriads of helpful hints to make housework quicker and less odious, from removing stains in the laundry to getting your children to help you around the house.

All of this — and much more — is in **PARENT TRICKS-OF-THE-TRADE.** Make your job easier with these 1,001 child-tested solutions that can make being a parent much more fun!

Kathleen Touw

Kathleen Touw, a former high school teacher, is now the experienced mother of Steven and Sara, aged five and 21 months, respectively.

Loel Barr

Loel Barr is a freelance illustrator and mother of Jessica and Alexander, aged five and 21 months. She has illustrated previous books, and contributes regularly to *The Washington Post.*

ISBN 87491-086-2/$9.95 hardcover
ISBN 87491-445-0/$4.95 quality paper, spiral bound
150 pages, fully illustrated, index, bibliography

ACROPOLIS BOOKS LTD.,   2400 17th St. N.W.,   Washington, D.C. 20009,   202-387-6805

The Father Book

Pregnancy and Beyond

by Rae Grad, R.N., Ph.D.; Deborah Bash, C.N.M.,;
Ruth Guyer, Ph.D.; Zoila Acevedo, R.N., Ph.D.;
Mary Anne Trause, Ph.D.; Diane Reukauf, M.A.

Written by the six founding members of the Alliance for Perinatal Research and Services, Inc., *The Father Book* is a thorough, easy-to-read, and sympathetic guide for fathers. It tells fathers all about the biology, issues and joys of pregnancy, childbirth and fatherhood.

More and more doctors have become convinced that the father is as important as the mother to a successful pregnancy and childbirth. His participation during the miracle of birth makes for much stronger family ties. But most childbirth books are written for the mother.

The Father Book was written just for the father to . . .

- provide a practical pregnancy and childbirth guide, aimed directly at his mental and physical needs, as well as to understanding those of his partner

- familiarize him with the issues in the contemporary childbirth experience, so he can make informed decisions

- acquaint him with the experiences, philosophies, concerns and feelings of other men who have become fathers

- provide him with information and advice for after the child is born.

The Father Book includes a glossary of commonly used pregnancy and childbirth terms and a directory of organizations interested in childbirth.

The Alliance for Perinatal Research and Services, Inc.

The six members of the Alliance are a multidisciplinary group, who are professionally involved with childbirth issues. They include a neonatal psychologist, a counselor, an immunologist, a nurse-midwife, nurses, health-educators and childbirth educators. This is their first book together.

ISBN 87491-618-6/$17.50 hardcover
ISBN 87491-422-1/$8.95 quality paper
225 pages, 8 x 9, illustrations, photos, index

ACROPOLIS BOOKS LTD.,   2400 17th St. N.W.,   Washington, D.C. 20009,   202-387-6805

Suggested Reading
Available at bookstores everywhere

If unavailable through your bookseller, you may order directly from the publisher, Acropolis Books, Ltd.

Listening Games

92 Listening & Thinking Activities

by Margaret John Maxwell

Listening is one of the most vital of all learning skills, but most children never really learn how. And, when you consider that they spend 50 to 75% of their classroom time listening to what their teacher is teaching, it's obvious that **LISTENING GAMES** is a much-needed book.

Listening abilities are learned, and **LISTENING GAMES** provides parents and teachers with 92 fun games and activities they can play with children to teach them how. These games can be played at home, in the car, in the classroom. Little or no materials, besides this book, are needed. The games are geared to preschool through elementary school, for groups or individuals.

Experienced teacher, Margaret John Maxwell, wrote **LISTENING GAMES** to provide enjoyable learning experiences for her students. Here she shares them with parents and other teachers. Use them as a reward for other less "fun" activities!

ISBN 87491-619-4/$9.95 quality paper
208 pages, 8-1/2 x 11, illustrated

Model of the United States Capitol

rendered by Robert Merritt

History comes alive when children put together this exact scaled replica of the U.S. Capitol — "the symbol of the power of the people," praised Nathaniel Hawthorne after a visit in 1862.

Now today's children can discover the fascinating history of this beautiful building, as they reconstruct its seven sections, the first begun in 1793, the last just completed in 1962.

Die-cut for easy assembly, this intriguing kit contains 1 in. to 32 ft. scaled parts for building a 24 in x 8-1/2 in. x 9 in. Capitol building. Complete with illustrated instructions and historical accounts, it makes an exciting educational activity for children 12 years and up (and that includes you!).

ISBN 87491-469-8/$11.95 per kit

ACROPOLIS BOOKS LTD.,   2400 17th St. N.W.,   Washington, D.C. 20009,   202-387-6805

Suggested Reading
Available at bookstores everywhere

If unavailable through your bookseller, you may order
directly from the publisher, Acropolis Books, Ltd.

Why Back-To-Basics Won't Work

How Education Could Develop
Children's Intelligence
Results of a Survey of 120,000 School Children
in 315 public, private and parochial schools
in 12 states

by Robert E. Bills, Ed.D.

"**S**omething terrible is happening to our children," says this respected educator. "No matter how hard schools try, and they are trying, today's kids don't seem to be getting as much out of school as we expect them to."

WHY BACK-TO-BASICS WON'T WORK is Dr. Bills' probing exploration of our children's education and what it is doing to them. It is based on his exhaustive survey of 120,000 school age children in 315 public, private and parochial schools, located in twelve states around the nation. And it proves that the longer students remain in school, the more they reject values such as honesty, trustworthiness, reliability, truthfulness, sincerity, cooperation and others vital to the survival of our society.

But it's not all the fault of the schools, Dr. Bills insists. The federal government and parents themselves have put unwarranted demands on schools, shifting their support from one program to another, without fully analyzing the results of these educational and social experiments on the children.

"In fact," concludes Dr. Bills, "The problem with today's schools is not that they are failing to teach enough 'basics,' but that they are failing to teach children how to 'behave intelligently,' to enable them to survive in a rapidly changing society."

WHY BACK-TO-BASICS WON'T WORK examines the real meaning of intelligence and offers a program for change that would help everyone expand their given intelligence to its limits.

Robert E. Bills, Ed.D.

Robert E. Bills is Research Professor and Dean Emeritus of the University of Alabama, and former Chairman of the Kentucky State Board of Examiners of Clinical Psychologists. Dr. Bills received his undergraduate and graduate degrees at the University of Kentucky and doctorate in clinical psychology at Columbia University's Teachers College. He is a Fellow of the American Psychological Association and Appears in *Who's Who in America*. Dr. Bills is the author of more than 100 books, abstracts, articles and studies.

ISBN 87491-430-2/$12.50 hardcover
300 pages, 6 x 9, index

ACROPOLIS BOOKS LTD.,   2400 17th St. N.W.,   Washington, D.C. 20009,   202-387-6805

Notes

Notes

Notes

Notes